THE PANIC OF 1857

THE PANIC OF 1857

AN ANALYTICAL STUDY

GEORGE W. VAN VLECK

NEW YORK

COLUMBIA UNIVERSITY PRESS

1943

Foreign Agents: OXFORD UNIVERSITY PRESS, Humphrey Milford, Amen House, London, E.C. 4, England, AND B. I. Building, Nicol Road, Bombay, India

MANUFACTURED IN THE UNITED STATES OF AMERICA

TO MY WIFE

PREFACE

IF THE investigation of economic history has taught anything in the past twenty or thirty years, it has shown that practically any economic movement of importance is an extremely complex phenomenon. The crisis of 1857 is by no means an exception to this rule. For this reason any investigator who approaches this problem must have clearly in mind at the outset just what he intends to do in his study. Two possible approaches are indicated. One is the descriptive approach —that is, a detailed day-by-day account of the development of the crisis, of the period of the panic, and finally of the post-panic readjustment. This would entail the accumulation of complete information on the daily business life of the period. Prices, market conditions, crop yields, banking conditions would have to be described as they fluctuated from week to week. Such a study, obviously valuable in its own right, would be a complete record of the crisis of 1857, but not an explanation of it.

The second approach to the problem is the analytical one. In this case, data and statistics would not constitute the bulk of the material contained in the study. Only so much of the daily movements of business conditions would be included as would serve to indicate the determining factors of the crisis. But here another difficulty presents itself. At what point in the economic life of the 1850's should the study begin and at what point should it end? What are the relevant factors and how may they be recognized? The economic life of a nation is a continuous, articulated organic whole which is ever developing out of itself. How can the fabric be artificially cut at any point and a part of it held up for examination without fundamentally distorting the whole?

Since this investigation of the crisis of 1857 is largely concerned with analysis rather than description, these problems must be faced. For this purpose this study has been divided into four parts. The first to be dealt with will be the long-term factors—those continuous weak spots within the organized structure of economic life whose aggravation or melioration bring the economic cycle round full circle. Specifically, the structure of American foreign and domestic commerce will be described; the banking and credit structure will be analyzed in an effort to understand the various stresses and strains to which it was liable; and finally the central position of Great Britain in world economy will be discussed.

Second, the short-term factors will be considered—those events happening within or without the American economic system during the years immediately before 1857 which served to aggravate the fundamental weaknesses of the economic structure and finally to bring the whole thing tumbling down in the panic of September, 1857. Under this heading notice will be taken not only of economic developments but also of political and social changes which reacted unfavorably on business conditions.

Third, a short account of the panic and crisis will be given with special reference to those phenomena which differentiate it from previous crises in American history.

Last, a brief analysis will be made of those forces operating during the fall of 1857 and the spring of 1858 which brought the crisis to an end and placed the American economic system on the path to a new prosperity.

My obligations in the preparation of the pages which follow have been many. I desire to express my sincere gratitude to Dr. Harry J. Carman of Columbia University, under whose direction this study has been carried on, and whose genuine friendship and helpful advice have contributed in large measure to the completion of the work. I take pleasure in acknowledging my indebtedness for their constructive criticism to

Professors John A. Krout, Allan Nevins, and Dwight C. Miner of the Department of History, and to Professors Joseph Dorfman and Arthur R. Burns of the Department of Economics, all of Columbia University. Mr. Theodore Geiger of the War Production Board staff has also been generous of his time and thought. To Dr. Joseph D. Allen, headmaster of the Poly Prep Country Day School of Brooklyn, New York, I am grateful for his sincere interest in my behalf. I am particularly grateful to my nephew, Howard W. Kramer, for his scholarly assistance in many ways; to my sister, Nellie E. Van Vleck, for her helpful cöoperation; to the staffs of the Library of Congress, Columbia University Library, the Brooklyn Public Library, and the New York Public Library for access to material and their many courtesies. To my wife, Jessie, by whom the tedious task of preparing the original manuscript for the publishers was performed and whose encouragement and counsel have been my constant inspiration, I am under lasting obligation. I alone assume responsibility for any errors of fact or interpretation which may appear in the text.

G. W. Van V.

New York
August, 1942

CONTENTS

CHAPTER ONE

THE STRUCTURE OF AMERICAN ECONOMY

THE YEAR 1857 found the United States in the midst of the greatest economic transformation in its history. This transformation took two forms. First, the shift within the economic system from agriculture to industry, which had begun with the nineteenth century, was already far enough advanced to mark the United States as one of the leading manufacturing nations of the world.[1] Second, within agriculture itself, the last vestiges of self-sustaining household production were being swept away as the production of crops for sale in a world market became the general practice in most regions of the country. Both of these transformations were, of course, mutually interrelated. Production for sale in agriculture meant an immeasurably larger market for the products of industry, and, conversely, the growth of industry created a greater demand for the products of the soil. Both aspects of this fundamental transformation might be summed up by saying that production for the market almost completely superseded production for home or local consumption.

Nevertheless, agriculture still supported most of the population of the United States during the 1850's, but it had become largely a commercial agriculture.[2] True enough, America produced its commercial crops even in the seventeenth and eighteenth centuries. Prior to the 1820's tobacco was produced almost exclusively for sale, and those general farming regions

[1] Total American manufactures in 1850 were $1,019,106,616 and in 1860 were $1,885,861,676. *Report of the 8th Census, Manufactures*, pp. 729–30.

[2] Thorp, *The Population of the United States*, p. 25.

with easy access to the seaports of Boston, New York, Philadelphia, Baltimore, and New Orleans shipped grain and cattle to the West Indies, South America, and the Mediterranean countries. But this early commercial agriculture was limited to certain specific regions of the country and did not comprise the overwhelming bulk of the agricultural products of the United States. With the real development of the market for cotton from the 1820's on, the qualitative transformation of American agriculture definitely began, and each decade thereafter saw an accelerated increase of agricultural production for sale abroad and in this country. Cotton sales abroad averaged about $25,000,000 during the 1820's; by the 1840's they were approximately $50,000,000 annually; by 1851 they crossed the $100,000,000 mark and within another ten years had almost reached $200,000,000 ($191,806,555 in 1860).[8] This unprecedented growth transformed the entire agriculture of the South. The non-slaveowning and non-cotton or tobacco-producing farmers of the South, who had previously raised corn and hogs mainly for their own consumption, now produced largely for sale to the plantation owners, who no longer attempted to grow enough food for their own slaves. Except for the mountainous country and lowest strata of the poor whites, agriculture in the South was almost completely commercialized by the 1850's.

The free farming regions of the Northeast and of the West experienced their great transformation from the 1840's on. The market abroad for American foodstuffs was a fairly constant one during the 1820's and 1830's, averaging about $12,000,000 a year until 1840. First the Irish famine, then the repeal of the English Corn Laws, and last the beginnings of industrialism in France and Germany after 1850 created a new demand for American grain. From a low of $9,588,359 in 1837, exports of foodstuffs rose to $68,701,921 in 1847 and

[8] *Report on the Finances,* Executive Document 2, 2d Sess., 36th Cong., pp. 416–17 [hereafter cited as 2:2:36].

reached a pre-Civil War high of $77,187,301 in 1856.[4] At the same time, the domestic market for grain was increasing as manufacturing developed and the population of the cities grew. Persons engaged in manufacturing and mechanical trades, in other words nonagricultural producers, constituted only 14 percent of the total population in 1820, but amounted to 25 percent in 1860.[5] Urban settlements (8,000 inhabitants or more) contained only 4.9 percent of the population in 1820, but by 1860 they contained over 16 percent.[6] Nevertheless, the growing foreign demand provided the most important increases in the market for food products.

Those who produce for sale are *ipso facto* forced to buy, and the more the farmers and planters of America sold their crops, the greater the demand for manufactured goods. At first, the market demand was met by the importation of foreign manufactures, in large part from England. But from the period of the War of 1812 on American manufacturing increased at a steady pace. Reliable statistics for the early period are lacking, and it is impossible to tell just at what point American manufacturers were able to supply the bulk of the demand for particular articles. But by the 1840's, when industrialization had already placed a definite stamp upon certain regions of the North Atlantic and New England States, the relative importance of American production as compared with foreign importation was becoming apparent. As early as 1831 cotton mills in twelve states of the Union produced over 230,000,000 yards of cotton cloth valued at approximately $26,000,000.[7] In the same year American imports of cotton goods from England totaled about $10,000,000.[8] By 1840 the disparity between domestic production and foreign importation of cotton goods was even greater. Cotton manufactures were estimated at over $46,000,000, while total imports of cotton goods fell to $6,500,-

[4] *Report on the Finances*, 2:2:36, p. 415. [5] Thorp, p. 25. [6] Thorp, p. 24.

[7] Timothy Pitkin, *A Statistical View of the Commerce of the United States*, p. 526.

[8] Pitkin, p. 395.

000, about $5,500,000 of which came from England.[9] In 1850 American production of cotton goods rose to over $65,000,000 and foreign imports to $19,000,000, the corresponding figures for 1860 being $115,000,000 and $9,000,000.[10] The ratio of increase of domestic manufactures of cotton was much greater than the ratio of increase of foreign imports, and by 1860 domestic producers controlled over three fourths of the total market for cotton goods as compared with about two thirds in 1831. In point of fact, American manufacturers dominated the market for cheaper cotton goods, while the English supplied the demand for expensive cottons.[11]

The woolen industry experienced a development less favorable to domestic producers than did the cotton manufacturing industry. In 1840 domestic woolen manufactures totaled over $20,000,000 and foreign importations were approximately $9,000,000, of which almost two thirds came from Great Britain.[12] By 1860 American production had risen to about $61,000,000 and foreign imports to $37,000,000.[13] However, the proportion of the market controlled by each was still the same, two to one.

A more impressive picture is presented by other branches of industry. The iron and steel industry, which in 1850 was producing far less than two thirds of the total output, raised its share to well over two thirds within ten years.[14] In the manufacture of boots and shoes, of hats and caps, of leather goods,

[9] John Macgregor, *Commercial Tariffs and Regulations, Resources and Trade of the United States*, II, 757–58, 1013–14.

[10] *Report of the 8th Census, Manufactures*, p. ix; *Report on the Finances*, 2:2:36, p. 406. The figure for cotton imports for 1860 is abnormally low and not representative of the decade from 1850 to 1860. Cotton imports in 1858 were $28,000,000 and in 1859 were $26,000,000. *Report on the Finances*, 2:2:36, p. 406.

[11] This was the case very definitely as early as 1842. American manufacturers in seven states printed over 100,000,000 yards of cotton goods, having a total value of $11,000,000. Only 8,000,000 yards were imported from England, with a total value of $5,000,000. Macgregor, II, 722–23.

[12] Macgregor, II, 757–58, 1013–14.

[13] *8th Census, Manufactures*, p. xxii; *Report on the Finances*, 2:2:36, p. 406.

[14] *8th Census, Manufactures*, p. clxxviii; *Report on the Finances*, 2:2:36, p. 406.

of hardware and cutlery, of agricultural implements, of furniture, of steam engines and machinery, of ready-made articles of clothing, American producers supplied over 90 percent of the domestic demand by 1860.[15] Nevertheless, throughout the pre-Civil War period there remained certain items of manufacture in which foreign producers dominated. Chief among these was the silk industry, in which American production was negligible.

Despite the successes of American industry in supplying more and more of the home demand, foreign imports rose steadily throughout the pre-Civil War period. During the 1820's foreign imports averaged about $80,000,000 a year, making a per capita consumption of foreign goods of about $5. By 1850 foreign imports were over $178,000,000, with a per capita consumption of $7. In 1857 a pre-Civil War high of $360,000,000 was reached, making a per capita consumption of almost $12.[16] The fact that per capita consumption of foreign goods increased two and a half times in thirty years gives some indication of the extent to which the inhabitants of the United States were becoming more and more dependent upon the market for the things they needed and consequently the extent to which they themselves were becoming producers of goods for sale, both in industry and in agriculture. If it is also kept in mind that American manufacturing increased at a far greater rate than did the importation of foreign goods, this figure of two and a half times must be raised to about six or seven times if a more accurate picture of American consumption of commodities is to be gained. Since the rate of increase of the urban population was by no means as large as this, it points once again to a great growth of commercial agriculture during the 1840's and 1850's.[17]

15 *8th Census, Manufactures*, pp. lx–lxv, lxvii–lxviii, lxxxii–lxxxvi; cliv–clxii; cxc–cxcii; cciv–ccxvii; clxxxviii. *Report on Commerce and Navigation*, Senate Documents, 2d Sess., 36th Cong., VIII, 172–305.

16 *Report on the Finances*, 2:2:36, p. 398.

17 This being the case, any disturbance in the normal exchange of commodi-

The symptoms of the crisis of 1857 first manifested themselves in the great commercial and financial centers of the eastern seaboard, and it was there, in fact, that the chief events of the panic were enacted. The agricultural hinterlands of the South and the West were dependent upon developments in New York, Boston, and Philadelphia and were responsive to them. Attention must therefore be focused upon the great centers of distribution and of credit, especially New York, which were the nerves of the economic structure. They responded most readily to changes in the world economic picture and were the channels through which the agricultural and manufacturing districts were affected.

Some indication of the paramount position which the great maritime centers occupied within the national economy can be seen from the accompanying chart, which shows the volume of goods which passed through them during the year ending June 30, 1857.[18]

Port	*Foreign Imports*	*Reëxports*	*Domestic Exports*
New York	$222,550,307	$13,360,384	$111,029,083
Boston	44,840,083	3,432,899	24,894,019
New Orleans	24,891,368	356,491	91,536,546
Philadelphia	17,850,630	169,920	6,965,236
Baltimore	10,581,208	300,942	13,405,393
San Francisco	9,130,698	2,225,182	12,210,719
Charleston	2,016,734		15,993,506
Savannah	779,909		10,670,273
Mobile	709,090		20,575,987

ties would have affected a far greater proportion of the population and affected them more deeply than was the case during the 1820's and 1830's. The crisis of 1857, therefore, has the dubious distinction of being the first modern crisis in American history from the point of view of the suffering it entailed. That a full-scale major economic depression was delayed until the 1870's by no means detracts from the importance of the crisis of 1857. Factors largely external to the American scene intervened to make the depression of short duration. But, in any case, America was fully as liable to a long economic depression during the late 1850's as it was during the 1870's.

[18] *Report on Commerce and Navigation,* Senate Documents, 1st Sess., 35th Cong., XIV, 324–25, 368, 486.

Over 90 percent of the trade entering or leaving the United States passed through these nine ports. New York alone handled 60 percent of all American imports and 33⅓ percent of all American exports, in addition to over half of the reëxports. Nor was it only foreign trade which created the commercial importance of New York, Boston, and Philadelphia. Over 90 percent of the manufactures of the United States was shipped from the factories to these cities for sale. This was especially true of the textile industry, centered as it was in Massachusetts, Rhode Island, Connecticut, and New York.[19]

The merchandise which left the chief seaports of the United States for all parts of the world was mainly raw materials. Throughout the decade of the 1850's cotton constituted more than half of American exports and with foodstuffs and tobacco made up more than three fourths of the total American exports, excluding specie. American manufactured goods to the value of $29,000,000 were shipped abroad in 1857 and constituted the next largest item of the export trade. Lumber and forest products, fish and whale oil, and certain miscellaneous raw materials completed the total of America's foreign exports.[20]

The largest single customer of the United States was Great Britain, which in 1857 took almost half of the total American exports. The three great staples—cotton, tobacco, and foodstuffs—together made up 90 percent of England's imports from the United States. Next in order of importance came France and its colonial possessions. Spain and its colonies came third, with Cuba alone taking over half of this amount. Altogether, the three great imperial powers and their colonies took over three fourths of the total American exports. The nations

19 See Ex. Doc. 6, 1st Sess., 29th Cong., II, 201–936, which contains answers to questionnaires sent to American manufacturers on the proposed tariff act of 1846. Over 90 percent of the manufacturers replying specify New York, Boston, and Philadelphia as the places to which their production was sent for sale.

20 *Report on the Finances*, 2:2:36, p. 401.

of South and Central America accounted for over half the remaining quarter, and the rest was divided among Germany, the Russian empire, China, Italy, Austria, and the Scandinavian states.[21]

A nearly similar division of the import trade of the United States existed in 1857. England alone, excluding Scotland and Ireland, sent more than one third of all the goods imported into the United States. If to this is added the value of the English goods shipped indirectly to the United States via Canada and of the exports of the rest of the British Empire, it would amount to half of the total American imports. The great bulk of the imports coming directly or indirectly from the British Isles consisted of manufactures of cotton, wool silk, and linen and also of iron and steel products. The English colonies sent raw materials. From France came approximately one seventh of the American imports, mainly silk textiles and luxury products. Spain itself shipped little to the United States, its exports amounting in 1857 to about $5,000,000. But the two Spanish colonies of Cuba and Puerto Rico exported sugar, molasses, tobacco, and cigars to the United States, totaling over $51,000,000 in the same year. This figure was greater than the imports from France and all its colonies Over $40,000,000 worth of raw materials were imported from Mexico, Central America, and South America, Brazil alone sending $21,000,000 worth of coffee, rubber, and tropical woods. China, Germany, and the other nations of Europe divided the remaining American imports, amounting to about $45,000,000 in 1857.[22]

The following table gives some idea of the extent of American foreign commerce for the years from 1850 to 1858 inclusive:[23]

[21] *Report on Commerce and Navigation*, 1st Sess., 35th Cong., Senate Documents, XIV, 50.

[22] *Ibid.*, pp. 268–69.

[23] *Report on the Finances*, 2:2:36, p. 316.

Year	*Total Imports Including Specie*	*Imports Entered for Domestic Consumption Excluding Specie*	*Domestic Produce Exported Excluding Specie*	*Foreign Reëxports Excluding Specie*	*Total Exports Including Specie*
1850	178,138,318	164,032,033	134,900,233	9,475,493	151,898,720
1851	216,224,932	200,476,219	178,620,138	10,295,121	218,388,011
1852	212,945,442	195,072,095	154,931,147	12,037,043	209,641,625
1853	267,978,647	251,071,358	189,869,162	13,096,213	230,452,250
1854	304,562,381	275,955,893	215,156,304	21,648,304	278,241,064
1855	261,468,520	231,650,340	192,751,135	26,158,368	275,156,846
1856	314,639,942	295,650,938	266,438,051	14,781,372	326,964,908
1857	360,890,141	333,511,295	278,906,713	14,917,046	362,960,682
1858	282,613,150	242,678,413	251,351,033	20,660,241	324,644,421

The American import trade from Great Britain was not only the largest part of the total imports of the United States, but it was a model on which the commerce with other foreign countries was based. Also, as will be seen later, American trade with nations other than Great Britain was to a considerable extent financed from London. For these reasons consideration of British-American trade relations is of first importance.

As many as six transactions from manufacturer to consumer can be distinguished in the American import trade with Great Britain during the 1850's. This figure represents a maximum which in some instances might be abridged by the omission of one or more steps in the process. English manufacturers producing for the American market designed to sell their goods primarily during two seasons of the year. There was one buying season during the early winter and a second, more important one, during the late spring months.[24] English manufacturers sold either directly to American importing merchants or to English exporters who in turn sold to the American importer. The American importing merchant made his purchases, therefore, from either of these two sources, but in a variety of ways. In case he bought directly from the English manufacturer, purchases were usually made in England by the American importer himself, by an agent resident in England

[24] New York *Tribune,* April 4, 1857.

for that purpose, or by mail order. If he purchased from an English exporting merchant, he usually bought by mail order. A relatively small quantity of goods was exported directly to the United States by English manufacturers or merchants either for sale on their own account or on consignment.[25]

The American importing merchant, however he acquired his stock, usually bought in large quantities and in turn wished to dispose of his goods in large lots. Most of his sales were accordingly made to jobbers, whose function it was to break up the large lots into smaller parcels suitable for retailers in the East; to wholesalers; and in some cases to large retailers in the West and the South. The jobbers, moreover, maintained a constant supply of the leading articles of import all the year round in order to meet any sudden demand or to supply retailers' shortages.[26] Auctions at which jobbers made their purchases were still held, but this method of obtaining imported goods had greatly declined since the 1820's, with the decline of direct exporting by English merchants and manufacturers.[27]

The western and southern buyers of imported goods might be either large retailers who could afford to patronize the jobbers or wholesalers who in turn sold their merchandise in small lots to little retailers and peddlers back home. In this way imported goods finally found their way into the hands of the ultimate consumers. As many as six transactions could thus intervene between the foreign manufacturers and the American consumers.

The structure of the exporting trade was almost as complex. Cotton and tobacco planters in the South generally sold their crops to the cotton and tobacco factors of New York, New Orleans, or Richmond, who had branch offices or agents at the chief collecting points of the South. In turn, the factors sold

25 Norman S. Buck, *The Development of the Organisation of Anglo-American Trade*, pp. 28–29.

26 Buck, pp. 84–85, 160.

27 *Hunt's Merchants' Magazine*, XXXII, 91.

the staples in the leading seaports of the South to a variety of customers. In the case of cotton, it might be bought by (1) northern merchants who supplied American spinners with their raw material; (2) foreign importers who maintained representatives in the cotton ports or empowered American agents to act for them; (3) American exporters who shipped on their own account or on consignment to foreign agents and brokers. It was to the second class of buyers that the largest portion of the cotton crop was finally disposed of.[28]

Grain-producing farmers in the West generally sold their produce to grain merchants located at the chief river and canal ports or at railroad towns. The grain moved by inland waterways to New York or New Orleans, where it was sold for export to much the same sort of purchasers as the cotton crop. Similar systems of export organization existed for the other raw materials sent out of the United States.[29]

The active impulse to the export of American manufactures and the reëxport of foreign manufactures, except those destined for Canada, came from American merchants rather than from their foreign customers. The chief markets for American manufactured goods were in South and Central America, the West Indies, and Africa, where among other purposes these goods were destined for the illegal slave trade. American merchants and shippers exported what they thought could be sold in those regions, and the transactions were usually entrusted to agents or representatives in the ports or to the captains and supercargoes of the vessels.[30]

English manufacturers and English exporters customarily gave long credits to the American importing merchants who purchased from them. Credits varied in length from six to eighteen months, and under normal circumstances renewals for additional periods could be obtained with little difficulty. In some instances American buyers paid for their purchases

28 Buck, pp. 84–85. 29 *Hunt's Merchants' Magazine*, 32, 91.
30 Manchester, Alan K., *British Preeminence in Brazil*, p. 314.

immediately by means of letters of credit which they brought with them to England. These were granted by British banking houses or their agents in America and were repaid by American merchants within the year. In either case American importing merchants were able to give long credits to the jobbers who bought from them. In their turn, the jobbers granted credits of from eight to eighteen months to the western and the southern merchants and shorter credits to the eastern retailers. Shopkeepers and retailers throughout the country received long credits from the wholesalers who served them. The planters and farmers who bought from the retailers usually obtained credits running until the next crop was marketed. The chain of credits thus rested for final payment upon the sale of a crop which in some cases might not yet be in the ground and the marketing of which in any case was a thing of the uncertain future. Final payments might take two years or even more, and the whole chain of indebtedness was sustained, if necessary, by frequent renewals of notes at every point from manufacturer to ultimate consumer.[31]

Conditions were much the same in the export trade, but in reverse. That is to say, the American planters and farmers usually received cash for their products, either in the form of credits against their debts on the books of their factors or in notes drawn on cotton factors and grain merchants. These were easily converted into cash by discounting at local or New York banks. Cotton and grain exporters were paid in relatively short-term notes drawn on English importing houses or their banks. These were immediately discountable and even sold at a premium during some seasons of the year. In their turn, English importers were able to honor their notes within three to six months, and even on sight, by discounting their bills of lading or warehousing receipts at English banking

[31] London *Economist*, Jan. 11, 1851, p. 30; *Parliamentary Papers*, 1857–58, V (Joint Committee on the Bank Acts), 348; Buck, pp. 112, 114–17; *Hunt's Merchants' Magazine*, X, 76–77; Myers, Margaret G., *The New York Money Market*, p. 65.

houses or by discounting the notes of English firms to whom they sold American imports.[32]

In the case of the American export trade, therefore, credits became longer the further the commodities moved from the grower to the manufacturer. Furthermore, this chain was sustained by constant renewals which in normal times were almost automatic. But, unlike the financing of the import trade, final payment did not rest upon a future crop nor was the risk borne by the original seller. It was the English half of the chain of American exports—English importing merchants, cotton jobbers, grain merchants, and so forth, and ultimately the British banking system—which supported the whole process. Payment for these exports rested upon the ability of the English population to consume American grain and to market the textiles manufactured from American cotton.

However, this by no means completes the account of the indebtedness of American foreign commerce to English credit. Not only was American trade with the British Empire financed in the manner indicated above, but American exports and imports to other nations were partly dependent on English credit. This was especially true of those countries with which the United States had an unfavorable balance of trade. Brazil will serve as the outstanding example.

In 1857 American exports to Brazil totaled approximately $5,500,000, while imports from Brazil stood at about $21,500,000. Undoubtedly part of the unfavorable balance of approximately $16,000,000 was made up of invisible items such as shipping charges, insurance charges, profits of the American carrying trade between Brazil and other countries, and so forth. But the bulk of the unfavorable trade balance owed to Brazil was paid by means of the *favorable* English balance of trade with Brazil, amounting in 1857 to about £2,260,000. American merchants borrowed the proceeds of the sale of

32 *Parliamentary Papers*, 1857–58, V, 138–39, 335; W. T. C. King, *History of the London Discount Market*, pp. 123–24, 124–25; Buck, pp. 84–85.

English goods in Rio and other ports and used them to buy Brazilian goods for shipment to the United States. Payments to the English lenders were made by means of bills of exchange drawn on London and purchased upon the sale of Brazilian goods in the United States. In this manner England financed a large part of the American import trade from Brazil. A similar situation existed in the China trade and in the American trade with several European nations.[33]

The financing of both the import and the export trade of the United States thus rested in large measure upon the financial resources of Great Britain, and the smoothness and prosperity of the flow of goods to and from America depended ultimately upon the strength and stability of British financial institutions. The immediate point of contact between American foreign commerce and the British banking system came for the most part in the manufacturing centers and the seaports of Great Britain. There British manufacturers, merchants, and jobbers discounted the notes of their customers. Discounts were generally made by the so-called country banks —the banks of Liverpool, Glasgow, Manchester, and other commercial and manufacturing towns. Not only did these banks discount bills of exchange, but they also gave loans to importers upon bills of lading and warehousing receipts. In normal times credit facilities were seldom withheld, and little investigation was made of the reliability of borrowers.[34]

The liberal loan policy of the banks of the commercial and manufacturing cities was consequent upon the ready market these institutions found for all types of commercial paper in London. The London money market was a full grown exchange, equipped with large numbers of bill brokers, traders, discount houses, and other types of investors in commercial paper. The great bill brokerage houses of the capital com-

[33] *Report on Commerce and Navigation,* Senate Documents, Vol. XIV, 1st Sess., 35th Cong.; *Parliamentary Papers,* LX, 116, 326–38; Manchester, Alan K., *British Preeminence in Brazil,* p. 315.

[34] *Parliamentary Papers,* 1857–58, V, 335; King, pp. 123–24.

peted eagerly for the privilege of selling commercial paper for the Liverpool and the Manchester banks, requiring nothing more than the signatures of the country banks on the paper. The bill brokers, in turn, found little difficulty in disposing of this paper to discount houses, to private investors, and to the banks of the British agricultural regions, which usually had a surplus of funds above the requirements of their localities.[35]

The funds of the London discount houses, bill brokers, and traders were derived in large part from call money loans granted to them by the London banks upon the security of their portfolios of commercial paper. The great London joint-stock banks did little discounting of their own, but were mainly deposit banks, paying interest upon practically all deposits. As a result, they tended to invest their funds at call, especially since part of their deposits consisted of the reserves of the country bankers of both the agricultural and the commercial regions. The London money market, therefore, was able to indulge in a tremendous business in commercial paper with only an insignificant capital of its own, relying for most of its funds upon call money loans extended to it by the London deposit banks. So avid was the market for commercial paper when times were good that the agents of London bill brokers and discount houses scoured the manufacturing districts and the seaports for paper, urging on the country banks greater leniency in making initial discounts and encouraging merchants and manufacturers to engage in pyramiding, excessive borrowing, and unsafe practices.[36]

Ultimately and most especially in times of crisis this entire credit structure was dependent upon the Bank of England. Through its note-issuing policy, discount rate, special advances, and open-market operations the Bank of England was able in a variety of ways to control the market for commercial

[35] King, *Parliamentary Papers*, pp. 6, 27, 1857–58, V, 38–41.
[36] *Parliamentary Papers*, 1857–58, V, viii; King, p. 50.

paper and the ability of the banks to make initial discounts. The most direct manner was in the bank's practice of making initial discounts to merchants, especially to great trading corporations such as the East India Company, and in rediscounting for the London bill brokers and discount houses. It also lent funds at call to the money market upon the security of commercial paper. Although generally the bank's discount rate was higher than the market rate, the bank frequently made special advances to the money market at less than the bank's rate. During crises the power of the bank was really felt. It was the sole recourse of harassed bill brokers and discount houses hard pressed to meet their demand loans. At such times the Bank of England was able to strip the bill brokers, the discount houses, and even the banks of their best assets at abnormally high discount rates. It reaped a rich harvest when this sound commercial paper, which alone it would take, was liquidated in the ordinary course of events. Its influence might be felt even across the Atlantic, for a high bank rate not only could shift the exchanges in favor of England and attract specie from the United States, but, in the absence of other sources of credit, could injure American foreign trade by making money too dear.[37]

The American financial system was by no means as solidly founded or as integrated as was that of Great Britain, but a detailed consideration of its weaknesses must be left until the next chapter. Suffice it to say here that it was largely from the great commercial centers of New York, Boston, Philadelphia, and New Orleans that the American import and export trade was financed. The commercial banks discounted the notes of the jobbers for the importers and the notes of country merchants and wholesalers for the jobbers. In the country regions the local shopkeepers generally advanced credit from their

[37] *Parliamentary Papers,* 1857–58, V, 24–27, 50–52; Elmer Wood, *English Theories of Central Banking Control, 1819–1858,* pp. 3–9; Andreadès, A., *History of the Bank of England,* pp. 314–15.

own resources to farmers and planters and, if necessary, negotiated promissory notes at their local banks in order to meet their obligations until crops could be sold and their customers' debts liquidated.[38]

The export trade was similarly financed from New York and other commercial centers. Grain merchants and cotton factors paid for their purchases with drafts on New York, raised on their own capital or by loans from New York banks. Once initial purchases of grain or of cotton had been made, additional credits could be raised in New York on the security of the bills of lading or warehousing receipts, and thus new funds were obtained for further buying. By this time some of the crop would be sold to foreign importers, and drafts on London would serve to pay off previous loans or to secure new ones. What made funds so readily available in New York during normal times, therefore, was the fact that English drafts were generally in great demand in order to meet payments for English imports.[39]

In addition to their share of the foreign commerce of the United States, the banks of New York, New England, and Philadelphia were called upon to finance American industry and internal commerce. American manufacturers customarily shipped most of their goods to the great seaports, where they were sold directly, or indirectly by middlemen, to wholesalers, exporters, and retailers. Manufacturers discounted the notes of their customers in small amounts locally and the remainder in the large commercial cities. In turn the dealers who supplied the manufacturers with raw materials and machinery discounted in the same way.[40]

Although the New York money market was by no means as well developed as that of London, it obviously financed a considerable business. Funds to supply the market came from

[38] D. R. Dewey, *Financial History of the United States* (8th Ed.).
[39] Buck, pp. 84–85; Myers, pp. 207–8.
[40] See n. 19.

three principal sources. Most important were the New York commercial banks, which used their extensive deposits to discount bills and to make call loans on the security of bills, stocks, and bonds. Of the total savings bank deposits, averaging about $25,000,000 in 1857, a substantial portion was kept at interest in the commercial banks, which used this money for discounting and the call loan market. Country bankers kept large deposits in the New York banks in order to enjoy the interest and to have a reserve for the redemption of their notes. This money was also available to the market through the medium of the commercial banks.[41]

The second source of funds to the money market was the insurance companies, with a total capital of $75,000,000, a large part of which was invested in stocks and bonds and in the security loan market.[42]

The third source, and by no means an inconsiderable one before the panic of 1857, was English credit. The banks of Liverpool, Glasgow, and other commercial cities were constantly engaged throughout the 1850's in supplying funds for the discounting of American bills in New York. The Western Bank of Scotland and the City Bank of Scotland were the two chief banks engaged in this business during 1857. Their agents in New York sold to American merchants letters of credit drawn upon these banks and used the proceeds of these sales to invest in local bills until a favorable moment arrived for remitting to Great Britain. Some notion of the extent of this practice can be gained from the fact that at the time of its failure in the fall of 1857 the Western Bank of Scotland alone had more than $2,600,000 invested in local New York bills, held in New York by its agents—an amount, incidentally, almost equal to the excess of the bank's liabilities over its assets and representing one third of its total capital. Such investments by British banks in local New York financing give

[41] Myers, p. 41; Thomas P. Kettell, *Southern Wealth and Northern Profits*, pp. 49–50; Myers, pp. 93, 106, 115, 116–18.

[42] Myers, p. 41.

further evidence of the great dependence of American economic life upon that of Great Britain.[43]

The final subject which must be discussed in this analysis of the fundamental structure of American economy is the question of the seasonal stresses and strains to which the financial structure was peculiarly liable. The raw materials produced by American farmers and planters were sold during two principal seasons of the year. The selling period for cotton began during the late summer, reached its peak during the fall, and lasted in steadily diminishing volume until the early spring. Foodstuffs, on the other hand, did not have a continuous market. The first selling period for grain occurred during the fall and lasted until the internal waterways were closed by ice for the winter. While the canals and rivers were frozen, only enough grain to meet the domestic demand was moved by railroad in the years before the Civil War. The second selling period for grain began in late March or early April, as soon as the waterways were navigable, and lasted until the previous year's crop was exhausted. As a result of the movements of produce, therefore, credits for the South and the West were accumulated in New York during the fall months of the year and also during the spring. The result was a seasonal shift in the domestic exchange rates which ordinarily favored New York. Especially during the fall gold might actually be shipped from New York to New Orleans and other cotton ports to meet the cotton bills drawn against New York. The shift in domestic exchange rates might also be accentuated by grain bills which would assist in tipping the balance against New York during the same period. A part of the southern and the western demands against New York would appear in the form of balances due country banks, an item which was especially large during the fall and very liable to sudden withdrawal.[44]

[43] *Parliamentary Papers*, 1857–58, V, 214–15, 242, 244–45, 368–69.
[44] Buck, pp. 82–83; Myers, pp. 207–8.

The spring sales of grain were generally not large enough to shift the domestic exchanges in favor of the West at that season, especially since at the same time western merchants would be remitting to the East in payment for domestic and foreign manufactured goods. There were two buying seasons for manufactures. The smaller one occurred during the first few months of the year, when western and southern merchants bought goods in the East in anticipation of spring needs and the spring sales of grain. Once the waterways were open, a lull occurred in the country demand for manufactures. The second buying season, and by far the more important, came during the early summer months in anticipation of the fall sales of produce. At these periods of the year, therefore, the domestic exchanges would be heavily in favor of New York and gold would flow to the metropolis.[45]

The seasonal variations in domestic exchanges were closely linked to the foreign exchanges. Funds flowed abroad from New York principally during two seasons of the year. The less important period was during the spring buying season, when payments were made for goods imported to meet the spring demand. The more important time, however, was during the late spring and throughout the summer, when payments were made for imports to satisfy the much larger fall demand. On the other hand, sterling rates were lowest during the late fall and winter months, when cotton and grain were moving abroad, and they might dip again during the spring in the event that spring grain sales were large, although spring was normally a time of high sterling rates.[46]

As a result of the movements of both foreign and domestic exchange rates, the greatest strain upon the New York money market came at the end of the summer and during the fall, when money was either moving abroad to pay for foreign imports or moving into the interior to pay for grain and cotton.

[45] *Idem.*

[46] A. H. Cole, "Seasonal Variation in Sterling Exchange," *Journal of Economic and Business History,* II, 208–11; Myers, pp. 72–75.

This autumnal strain was always further aggravated by the fact that quarterly payments of all kinds occurred normally during August and November. Rents, interest, dividends, fees, premiums, and so forth were generally payable four times a year—in February, May, August, and November—and businessmen, private individuals, the United States Treasury, and the various state governments customarily withdrew large sums in cash from the money market to meet such obligations. The August quarterly payments coincided with the meeting point of the foreign and domestic strain upon the New York money market and made August the most difficult month of the year for the entire financial structure.[47]

From the foregoing analysis of the basic economic relations of the United States during the 1850's two main conclusions may be drawn. First and most striking is the deep-seated dependence of American economic life upon that of Great Britain. Not only were the British Isles the largest single market for American produce and the greatest single source of American imports, but the financing of America's foreign trade almost exclusively and of her domestic trade in part rested upon British credit. Nor can the sizable British long-term investments in American railroads, governmental obligations, and other securities, which will be discussed later, be ignored in this connection. Any disturbances to which the British economic structure was liable were bound to have their reactions in the United States. A study of the short-term fluctuations in British economic life during the period immediately prior to the crisis of 1857 is therefore decidedly pertinent and will be undertaken in a later chapter.

The second conclusion to be drawn is that there were inherent weaknesses in the American economic structure, arising from the basic relations within the country itself. A more detailed study of these, particularly as they relate to the financial and banking structure of the United States, is in order and will be the subject of the next chapter.

[47] Myers, p. 208.

CHAPTER TWO

THE BANKING SYSTEM, CREDIT, AND SPECULATION

IT HAS BEEN customary for both older writers and modern contemporaries to discuss the banking system of the United States before the Civil War chiefly in its aspect of supplier of the circulating medium.[1] This concentration upon the note-issuing theories and practices of American banking is understandable if only because of the spectacular and often disastrous events which formed the history of American banks of issue before the establishment of the national banking system. All too frequently discussion of the problem has been limited largely to sorting banks with sound issue policies from those with unsound ones and to tracing out the more dramatic successes and failures in detail. Yet such an attitude toward the history of American banking fails in two respects—it limits the field of inquiry to but one aspect of the banking and credit structure before the Civil War and it distorts the analysis of the causes and character of financial weakness during those years. Other aspects of banking are neglected or totally ignored, with the result that a static picture is obtained which never adequately portrays the internal relationships within the banking system or the relationship between the banks and the business community.

That there should have been during the period under review this one-sided interest in banks as issuers of the circulat-

[1] See, for example, Sumner, *History of Banking of All Nations*, Vol. I; Knox, *A History of Banking in the United States;* Dewey, *State Banking before the Civil War* and *Financial History of the United States*, among many others.

ing medium is quite understandable.[2] Despite the great industrial and commercial development of the United States during the 1850's, both in theory and in practice American banking was still orientated almost completely toward the needs of an agricultural economy. The principal function of banks, according to the dominant notion, was to serve primarily as banks of issue to provide a paper-money circulation and to pursue a liberal policy of lending out this money for agricultural needs. Only secondarily were banks thought of as institutions of deposit and discount. Experiments with a central banking system (the First and Second Banks of the United States), which inevitably led to the growth of deposit and discount functions, had long since been abandoned in the face of opposition from the numerically dominant agricultural sections of the country. Cheap money and extensive facilities for farm and chattel mortgages, crop loans, and advances to farmers and planters who wished to speculate in land or expand their acreage were the basic banking demands of the agricultural population. It was no wonder, then, that the fulfillment of these needs was the chief concern of American banking theory and practice in all sections of the country except the great commercial centers. How to attain a maximum circulation with—and unfortunately in many instances without—the greatest possible security for its redemption was the pressing question of American banking before the Civil War.

Yet it is significant that, with rare exceptions, the only sections in which a successful note-issue policy was achieved were precisely those regions where circulation was not the all-important aspect of banking. And it was precisely for that reason that banknote circulation policy was as successful as it was in New York, New England, Philadelphia, and New Orleans. By the 1850's, in and around New York, Boston, Philadelphia, and New Orleans, the banking system was almost

[2] For examples of this, see Miller, *Banking Theories in the United States before 1860*, pp. 16–17. An exception to this general attitude was that of Stephen Colwell, author of *Ways and Means of Payment*, New York, 1859.

completely adapted to commercial and industrial needs. The banks of these cities were chiefly engaged in receiving deposits and in making loans and discounts for business and governmental purposes. Banknote circulation was of secondary importance. Evidence of this may be seen in the banking statistics of the 1850's. During the years from 1850 to 1860 the banks of New York, Massachusetts, and Pennsylvania possessed one half of the banking capital of the nation, received over two thirds of all deposits, and made over one half of all loans and discounts. On the other hand, these banks issued less than one third of the total circulation of banknotes, although they owned one half of the specie in the possession of the banks. The note circulation of the New York, Massachusetts, and Pennsylvania banks was less than double their specie reserves, while the note circulation of all other banks was more than three times their specie reserves. Compared with this, in the commercial regions specie was less than one quarter of the total deposits, while in the agricultural regions specie was equal to one half of the total deposits.[3]

These percentages of average figures for the decade from 1850 to 1860 show clearly the fundamental bifurcation of the American banking system. Nor can these differences be explained merely by saying that the banks of the agricultural regions pursued an unsound circulation policy and a sound deposit policy while the banks of the commercial sections followed a sound circulation policy and an unsound deposit policy. The explanation lies rather in the basic economic differences within the country itself. The establishment of the New York Clearing House Association in 1853 is but further evidence of the fact that by this time the city banks were financing business needs chiefly from deposits and that loans and discounts appeared in the form of deposits rather than in the form of banknotes in circulation.[4] In other words, a modern

[3] *Preliminary Report of the Census*, 1860.

[4] See the account of banking practices in 1857 given in Gibbons, *The Banks of New York* [N.Y.], 1858.

type of banking system had replaced the older type in which loans were chiefly made by paying out notes. Yet the theory of the older banking system still dominated, and New York bankers thought themselves in an impregnable position in 1857 because of the high ratio which their specie reserves bore to their banknote circulation.[5] They were to learn to their dismay that the important ratio now was that between deposits and specie, for the "runs" which they experienced during the panic were in the form of deposit withdrawals and not demands for banknote redemption.[6] The crisis of 1857 made an important contribution to banking theory by bringing about the realization that banknote circulation was no longer the chief concern of bankers. The lesson of 1857 cleared the air for the reëxamination of the banking structure which led ultimately to the adoption of the national banking system.

The misfortunes of the older banking system—the "wildcat" banks, the exaggerated note issues, the dismal failure of state-supported institutions, the irresponsibility of private and corporate banks, the inadequacy of safety-fund schemes, and so forth—are all familiar stories and need not be repeated here. The relationship of the city banks to the business community has been discussed in Chapter One. But what requires more extensive treatment here is the relationship between the banks of the agricultural regions and those of the commercial regions. The balance of domestic payments generally favored New York throughout the year, and as a result large quantities of country banknotes were constantly arriving in the metropolis in payment for goods shipped to the South and the West.[7] The same was true, although to a much smaller extent, in the cases of Boston and Philadelphia. For their own protection the city banks were anxious to redeem country banknotes as quickly as possible, and for this purpose several devices were used in the period before the Civil War. Country banknotes were sent home for redemption, but this was an expensive and

[5] Myers, p. 92. [6] See below, Chapter Four. [7] See above, p. 19.

uncertain process and therefore avoided whenever possible. The most practical alternative was the Suffolk system employed in New England. The Suffolk Bank of Boston, in cooperation with other large city banks, maintained a fund for the purchase of country banknotes circulating below par in order to present these notes for immediate redemption at their banks of issue. Those country banks which consented to maintain a permanent deposit of $2,000 with the Suffolk Bank in addition to a sum sufficient for current redemptions would have their notes received at par by the Boston banks and would not be subject to constant calls for redemption. By means of this device the city banks could exercise some control over country banknotes, keep them at par, and force the country banks to assume the responsibility of their own note circulations.[8]

The banks of New York City had no formal organization such as the Suffolk system, but in general followed the same policy. By 1856 the supervision of country banknote circulation was in the hands of six large New York banks.[9] Country bankers were induced by the payment of 4 percent interest and the threat that otherwise their notes would be sent home for redemption to maintain permanent deposits in these New York banks.[10] Nor were the country banks reluctant to do this. In many instances they preferred to invest their funds at 4 percent interest on call with the New York banks rather than sink them for an indefinite period in agricultural mortgages. Naturally the New York banks encouraged this attitude and employed the country deposits in carrying on their regular banking business. During the late summer and early fall country deposits rose to large proportions because of the sales of cotton and foodstuffs. In the mid 1850's balances due to country bankers were as high as $35,000,000 during Septem-

[8] Conant, *A History of Modern Banks of Issue*, pp. 366–69.
[9] Myers, 116–18. [10] Dunbar, *Economic Essays*, p. 276.

ber and sank to $17,000,000 by winter as payments were made for manufactured goods.[11]

The weaknesses of the country banking system were quite evident. Most of the agricultural banks were chronically short of specie during the greater part of the year. As a result, many states permitted their banks to base their circulation not upon specie but upon holdings of securities. No matter how stringent were the requirements for the types of securities which could be held as collateral for banknotes, this system was certain to be severely strained during periods of declining security values. The other investments of these banks were far less liquid than were those of the city banks and in fact were liable to become frozen in times of stress. For this reason the country banks always considered their city deposits the most liquid portion of their assets and called for them first whenever trouble appeared.[12]

In normal times the banks of the commercial regions were able to take advantage of the weakness of the country banks in order to build up their own deposits and supervise country note issues. But when a crisis occurred, the difficulties of the city banks were aggravated by the weakness of the country banking system. Declining security values might force the country banks into complete suspension and in any case would compel the withdrawal of country deposits from New York, Boston, and Philadelphia. This would make the money market in those cities far more stringent than it was, just at a time when the demand for accommodations was steadily increasing and the panic could only be checked by the extension of additional loans. One effect of this situation would naturally be a further decline in security values as debtors sought frantically to turn their assets into money in order to meet

[11] Kettell, *Southern Wealth and Northern Profits*, pp. 49–50. Myers estimates that country bank deposits were one-quarter of the total deposits in the New York banks during the 1850's. Myers, p. 108.

[12] See below, Chapter Four.

loans which could no longer be renewed or extended. The net result was a vicious circle which might, and in 1857 did, contribute to the suspension of the city banks as well.[13] The weakness of the country banks was thus both a source of profit and a source of danger to the banks of New York, Boston, and Philadelphia.

The city banks were not immune from difficulties of their own. Chief of these was the perennial inadequacy of all nineteenth-century banking systems in the face of a crisis. As deposits and specie declined, the banks were naturally forced to curtail loans and discounts when the only way to stop the panic was to increase accommodations to the money market. Ultimately either suspension or failure faced the banks, and those who could avoid the second chose the first. In 1857 the arrival of this stage of the panic was hastened by the withdrawal of the country deposits and the declining values of the large amounts of railroad securities which the banks held.

The heavy commitments of railroad securities in the possession of the banks in 1857 were the result of the wave of speculation in land, stocks, and commodities which distinguished the decade and were but one aspect of the banks' connections with this speculative movement. The outstanding burden which the financial system of the United States had to bear throughout the entire pre-Civil War period was the national predilection for speculations of all sorts. The speculative wave of the 1850's was in every respect comparable to that of the 1830's. The high point was reached in 1856, but from that year until the fall of 1857 values held firm, speculation was still brisk, and participation still widespread. Some account of this wave of speculation must be given if its effect upon the banks is to be understood.

Writers on the subject of American speculation during this period are too often prone to treat it as another example of the supreme folly to which Americans were liable at times and

[13] See below, Chapter Four.

which could have been avoided if saner counsels and saner practices had prevailed.[14] But such an attitude toward the problem of speculation is a purely moral one and does not lead to an explanation. Only an inquiry which accepts the fact of speculation, as already given, as an organic part of the economic structure before the Civil War can hope to arrive at an understanding of that phenomenon.

Actually several sorts of speculation must be distinguished. As in any well-developed commercial society, there was normally considerable trading in commodities which varied in intensity as goods were in or out of season. Furthermore, financial organization had long since reached the point which necessitated permanent markets for public and private securities, commercial paper, mortgages, and short-term Treasury notes. With the exception of government bonds and railroad securities, neither of these two basic fields of speculation has been much commented upon. But that form of speculation which has commanded the most attention and which has been most often condemned as illegitimate and unnecessary was speculation in land. Its history was spectacular enough to attract attention, to be sure, but that was not its only *raison d'être.*

Basic to an understanding of American land speculation during the nineteenth century is the realization of the fact that it was by no means an unnatural phenomenon. The agricultural regions of the United States were in the process of constant expansion under the influence of a growing population and a widening market.[15] With seemingly limitless acres available for future cultivation, there was no incentive to practice an intensive agriculture except near the large urban centers. Extensive agriculture, with its attendant robbing of the soil, was therefore the general rule. Few farmers or planters could afford, in the face of the competition from

[14] See, for example, among others, Sakolski, *The Great American Land Bubble;* Hibbard, *A History of the Public Land Policies.*

[15] See above, pp. 2 ff.

newly opened lands, to invest in fertilizer, draining, ditching, fencing, or other improvements which might prolong or preserve the fertility of their soil. In general, after a certain point was reached it was more profitable to sell a farm or plantation to newcomers or abandon it altogether and move farther westward where virgin soil could be had in any case fairly cheaply and often without even the asking.

Among the slave owners, moving westward was all too frequently a matter of necessity and not of choice between a smaller or a larger profit. Cotton and tobacco exhausted the soil far more rapidly than did grain or corn. With a labor force representing a sizable capital investment, it was ruinous to continue to employ it upon lands which yielded an ever-diminishing return. When faced with the choice of improvement or removal, plantation owners were in a position to choose the former only under unusual conditions. Capital for improvements must be readily and cheaply available, and the cost and inconveniences of removal must be too great to warrant the sacrifice of especially advantageous transportation and marketing facilities in the old location. In the absence of these two factors—cheap capital and superior transportation—plantation owners, when they reached the point of diminishing returns, had their minds made up for them by circumstances beyond their control. Their only alternatives were to move westward or else to sell their slaves, who might be so encumbered with mortgages that they would yield little to their owners, although their price was constantly rising. Many, of course, did neither and sank deeper and deeper into decay until the Civil War put an end to their problems.

This westward movement, arising not only from the constant population increase but from the competitive nature of American agriculture itself, had as one of its most important consequences the creation of a permanent and ever-growing demand for land. And inevitably, whenever there is a constant and growing demand for a commodity, a market arises. Like the usual commodity market, the market for land was maintained by people who came merely to buy cheap and sell dear and by the ultimate users of this commodity, the farmers and planters themselves. Land speculators in the West and eastern investors in land there were in abundance, but the most numerous portion of the market were the farmers and planters. They were both "consumers" of land and speculators in it. They bought more than they cultivated—and by so doing they hedged against the declining value of the acres they planted; they paid off mortgages and loans from the proceeds of land sales after the region had become more settled and prices had normally risen; they provided themselves with a reserve to tide them over periods of low prices and crop failures; and they were always able to expand their cultivation in case labor should become more available or agricultural prices rose. But during boom times this more or less sound basis for acquiring excess lands was thrown to the winds. Farms were heavily mortgaged to permit the buying of more land, which in turn was mortgaged in order that the speculation might be pyramided still further. A collapse in land prices would wipe out thousands of farmers and transfer their holdings to the hands of professional speculators and banks.

Although the professional speculators numbered among their ranks Senators, Congressmen, Wall Street magnates, state and local officials, and gentlemen of the cloth, in addition to the regular crew of land sharks and promoters, the most important part during the wave of the 1850's was played by the railroads and the financiers who controlled them. Land grants to railroads by the federal government totaled more than 24,000,000 acres during the years from 1850 to 1857.[16] The outstanding example of governmental munificence before the Civil War was, of course, the land grant to the Illinois Central Railroad, which totaled one fourteenth of the state

[16] Senate Documents, 2d Sess., 36th Cong., Vol. I, p. 78.

of Illinois. By 1857 nearly half of this had already been disposed of at terms very advantageous to the railroad and its promoters.[17]

Although railroad lands and prospective town lots constituted the most popular speculation, the public domain was by no means neglected. Alienation of the public lands was made easier during the 1850's by the passage of the four general bounty bills between 1847 and 1855 and the adoption of the Graduation Act in 1854. In addition, in 1850 Congress granted to the states all the swamp and overflow land which lay within their borders, thereby swelling the amount which the states themselves could dispose of to railroads, speculators, and settlers. The following table gives some idea of the number of acres of public lands disposed of during the 1850's and the categories to which they went: [18]

Year Ending June 30	*Sold for Cash*	*Military Bounty Warrants and Other Warrants*	*Total per Annum*	*Swamp Grants to States*
1848 to 1851			under 5,000,000	
1852	1,553,071	3,316,996	4,870,067	5,219,188
1853	1,083,495	6,151,786	7,235,281	16,684,253
1854	7,035,735	3,416,802	10,452,537	11,033,813
1855	15,729,524	1,345,580	17,075,140	7,470,746
1856	9,227,878	8,382,480	17,610,358	6,036,874
1857	4,142,744	6,283,920	10,426,664	2,962,408
March 1, 1857, to Sept. 30, 1860	14,347,887	15,575,962	29,923,749	5,482,263

The peak of this great land boom came in 1855 and 1856. A contemporary estimate, undoubtedly much exaggerated, gives $800,000,000 as the sum invested in uncultivated land and unimproved town lots alone, three quarters of this being on credit without any cash transaction.[19] The actual sum was probably less than half this figure, but it serves to show the ex-

[17] Gates, *The Illinois Central Railroad and Its Colonization Work*, pp. 100 ff., 260.

[18] Table compiled from Executive Documents, 2d Sess., 32d Cong., I, 61; Ex. Doc. 1:33, Vol. I, p. 71; Ex. Doc. 2:33, Vol. I, p. 70; Ex. Doc. 1:34, Vol. I, pp. 140–41; Ex. Doc. 3:34, Vol. I, p. 191; Ex. Doc. 1:35, Vol. I, p. 80; 2:36, Senate Documents, Vol. I, p. 78.

[19] Mitchell, D. W., *Ten Years in the United States*, p. 328.

tent to which the banks must have been involved in the land speculations of the period. Even if they financed but a fraction of the total, the effect upon the banks of the collapse of the real estate boom can easily be imagined.

The immediate causes of the land boom of the 1850's are easily discernible. For the South, the decade was the most crucial one in the entire history of its "peculiar institution." Economically as well as politically the slave system was desperate during the 1850's. Slave prices were rising fast, out of all proportion to the rise in cotton prices.[20] Yet despite the increasing cost of labor the rise in cotton promised profits if the cost of production could still be kept low by the constant use of new, fertile land. Increased profits meant an easing of the ever-growing burden of commercial and financial dependence on the North, which was estimated to cost the South close to $65,000,000 annually in interest and brokerage charges alone.[21] Westward expansion seemed and was, for that matter, far easier of attainment than the reopening of the African slave trade or the breaking of the economic dependence on the North. It was no wonder, then, that southern planters were among the foremost in the ranks of the land speculators.

In the free West land speculation was not so much the result of desperation as it was of unrivaled prosperity. The prices of foodstuffs were rising, and the market for them constantly widening both at home and abroad. Population growth during the 1850's was greater than ever before, and railroad construction also reached a new height during the decade.[22] Not since the boom times of the 1830's had the West known such prosperity. On this basis speculation in the West far exceeded its normal limits and rose in a crescendo until the collapse of 1857.

20 For slave prices see Frederic Bancroft, *Slave-Trading in the Old South*, pp. 64, 339. For cotton prices see B. Phillips, *American Negro Slavery*, especially chart comparing slave and cotton prices.

21 Kettell, pp. 74–75.

22 From 1850 to 1860 railroad mileage grew from 8,589 miles to 30,793 miles. *Preliminary Report of the Census*, 1860.

As the London *Economist* warned, after tracing land speculation in the United States to the high prices of foodstuffs:

> The speculators hope, by securing a partial monopoly of the soil, favourable to the growth and carriage of corn, and to the increase of settlers, to obtain wealth from the pressing necessity to obtain more food. As a body, they will not succeed; their failure and the public injury are expected to be manifested in a money panic.[23]

The effects of this land speculation upon general business conditions just prior to the panic of 1857 will be discussed in a later chapter.

Although the great commercial centers were deeply involved in the western land boom, securities and commodities also commanded their speculative attention. Railroad financing became during the 1850's one of the major concerns of the city banks. Since the amount of state and local debts remained fairly constant until the crisis while the federal debt actually declined, the banks were forced to rely more and more upon the growth of railroad securities. As of June 30, 1857, there were outstanding approximately $500,000,000 of railroad stocks and $400,000,000 of short and long-term railroad bonds.[24] As railroad securities yielded anywhere from 5 to 10 percent, the banks were by no means reluctant to invest in them or to accept them as collateral, despite the slow but steady decline in railroad security prices from 1854 on.[25] Speculation was especially widespread in railroad stocks throughout the eastern markets, with the banks supplying funds liberally to brokers and traders. The causes of the decline in railroad securities and the extent of the banks' involvement in them will be discussed in a later chapter.

Evidences of commodity speculation are difficult to discover

23 London *Economist*, XV, 728–29, July 4, 1857.

24 *Report on the Finances*, I:35, p. 44. This table is only an approximation.

25 On railroad security yields see Reginald McGrane, *Foreign Bondholders and American State Debts*, p. 278. On railroad security prices during the 1850's see table in New York *Tribune*, June 20, 1857.

in the records of the period, but some indication of its extent can be gained from an editorial in the New York *Herald* of July 18, 1857. According to the writer, prices of virtually everything had increased fully 40 percent in four years, a condition which was attributed to "the spirit of reckless speculation that has swept over all portions of the country." This "artificial dearness of the necessities of life," the editorial said, had resulted in many "conscienceless speculators" making large fortunes while millions of consumers suffered. Continued the *Herald:*

> We have been furnished with some interesting particulars in relation to the effect which this speculative mania has had on two important products—sugar and cotton—both necessities of civilized life. As to sugar, all housekeepers are but too well aware of the high price at which it is maintained, compared with its price a few years since. And yet statistical evidence exists to show . . . that a price fifty percent less than that now paid would be remunerative. . . . The other article on which speculators have operated with still more disastrous results is cotton. Notwithstanding an estimated crop in the United States of about 3,000,000 bales, with a large supply from other quarters, and with fully 300,000 bales in the hands of manufacturers in Europe, prices have been raised four cents per pound over the rates current in this market last July; or, in other words, the price of cotton has advanced forty percent. Heavy brown sheetings, which were then dull at eight cents, are now quoted lifeless at nine to nine and a quarter cents, with a large accumulated stock. Some makes of goods are represented as being twenty and twenty-five percent larger in stock at the various agencies than they were at that date. Here is an advance of nearly forty percent in raw material, and only twelve to fifteen percent in the manufactured article.[26]

European investors were by no means reluctant to participate in the American economic upswing of the early 1850's. The unsettled political situation in Europe from 1847 on brought considerable continental funds to this country, al-

[26] New York *Herald,* July 18, 1857. The probable effect of the gold discoveries upon prices will be discussed later, as will the whole question of commodity

though no reliable estimates exist of the amount.[27] After 1850 English investors were able to look abroad once again and naturally were attracted by the American railway boom then developing. For the next few years American railroad securities were extremely popular in England and continued so until 1856, despite the temporary liquidation of foreign investments during the Crimean War.[28] The Parliamentary Select Committee on the Bank Acts and the Commercial Distress estimated the amount of American securities held in Great Britain on the eve of the crisis of 1857 at £80,000,000.[29]

This figure for English investments alone is considerably higher than contemporary American estimates of the total foreign holdings of American securities. In 1851 the New York *Times* reported that English investments in American long-term securities were $225,000,000.[30] Compared with this, in 1853 the United States Treasury estimated that the total European holdings in this country were only $222,000,000, although the amount was known to be higher than in 1851.[31] At the end of 1856 the Treasury maintained that foreign investments had risen to $240,000,000, but both the New York *Times* and the New York *Herald* protested that this figure was much too small.[32] *Hunt's Merchants' Magazine,* however, agreed with the Treasury and placed the total foreign investments in 1857 at $250,000,000, of which $160,000,000 represented railroad securities alone.[33] It is safe to conclude that the foreign holdings of American securities at the beginning of 1857 were somewhere between $250,000,000 and $350,000,000.

27 McGrane, *Foreign Bondholders and American State Debts,* p. 275.

28 D. M. Evans, *History of the Commercial Crisis,* p. 101. *American Bankers' Magazine,* N.S., IV, 79.

29 *Parliamentary Papers,* 1857–58, V, viii. Hobson, C. K., *The Export of Capital,* p. 40, mistakenly cites this figure as being for railroad securities alone, although the Committee expressly says otherwise.

30 New York *Times,* Nov. 25, 1851.

31 Ex. Doc., 2d Sess., 33d Cong., p. 42.

32 *Report on the Finances,* 1856; New York *Herald,* March 18, 1857; New York *Times,* March 19, 1857.

33 *Hunt's Merchants' Magazine,* XXXVIII, 21.

Within the ordinary credit system which financed the internal mercantile business of the United States there were also tendencies toward speculation. In addition to the over-expansion of mercantile and manufacturing enterprises, which will be discussed in a later chapter, many merchants and jobbers in the great commercial centers were investing their capital in, or borrowing funds for, speculation in commercial paper. Instead of discounting customers' notes at the banks or making collections when debts fell due, they preferred to enjoy the high money rates by holding their customers' paper themselves and renewing it indefinitely when it fell due. As a result the normal connection between commercial transactions and the commercial paper they were supposed to liquidate was lost. Debts were carried over from one year to the next, and in this manner short-term commercial paper, secured by the sale of goods, was converted into long-term investments without any security at all. On the eve of the crisis the leading mercantile agency in New York estimated the total internal mercantile debt of the United States to be in excess of $2,500,000,000.[34]

Thus by 1857 the entire banking and credit structure of the country was characterized by speculative practices and internal weaknesses which undermined the stability of the whole. It is necessary now to turn to those factors in world economy as a whole which combined to bring the entire structure tumbling down in the fall of 1857.

34 *Report of the Mercantile Agency*, B. Douglass & Co., New York, Jan., 1858.

CHAPTER THREE

SHORT-TERM FACTORS IN WORLD ECONOMY

THE OUTSTANDING development in world economy during the 1850's and one which was destined to have a deep influence upon the cycle of prosperity and depression during that decade was the large increase in the international stocks of gold as a result of the discoveries of gold in California and Australia. The unprecedented amounts of gold which became available for world economy during the early 1850's did much to relieve the acute specie shortage of the preceding decade. World economy and world population had been growing at a rapid rate, and available stocks of gold had not been increased sufficiently to prevent falling prices and specie shortages in many of the leading nations. The California gold discoveries of 1848 and the Australian gold discoveries of 1851 not only reversed this situation but created the monetary conditions necessary for the boom and the crisis of the 1850's.

The effect of the mid-century gold discoveries on prices is really a question of long-term factors. It is impossible to state with certainty whether the rising prices during the short period of nine years previous to the crisis were caused by the increase in specie, the "normal" price rise of a boom period, or a combination of both. In all likelihood the last was the case. Cassel and Kitchin agree that since 1850 when the annual gold increment has been more than 3 percent prices have risen and when less than 3 percent prices have fallen. In 1857 Tooke and Newmarch calculated the annual gold increment since 1848 as well over 5 percent per annum, but they concluded that this had no discernable effect upon prices. Rather, they argued, it had been absorbed in the tremendous expansion of foreign trade and in the unprecedented growth of capital goods investments.[1]

There can be no doubt, however, that the authors of *A History of Prices* were correct when they emphasized the consequences of the gold discoveries for the expansion of world economy. The increased credit and the facilities for international payments which the new gold made possible were the necessary preconditions for the unprecedented growth in world trade, industrial construction, and railroad building during the 1850's. Contrary to expectations, the gold increases were not attended by low money rates except for a brief period during 1852. In fact, interest rates were high during the greater part of the period before the crisis for reasons which will be discussed below.

One immediate effect of the gold discoveries was the upsetting of the gold-silver ratio. Several nations, notably France, were on a bimetallic standard, while early in the 1850's Holland, Belgium, and a number of the German states demonetized gold completely. Because of the fall in the value of gold, these silver standard nations had great difficulty in maintaining adequate reserves of silver, which tended to become hoarded in private hands. The results were continuous monetary difficulties in these countries throughout the 1850's which were aggravated by the drain of silver to the Far East.[2]

1 Tooke and Newmarch, *A History of Prices*, VI, 152–53, 230–36. This chapter is deeply indebted to Tooke and Newmarch. In fact, as J. H. Clapham wrote, "Very little has been written in any language about those aspects of economic history on which Tooke and Newmarch were specialists which does not come, directly or indirectly, from them." J. H. Clapham, *An Economic History of Modern Britain*, III, 366n. Like Clapham, the author prefers to cite *A History of Prices* directly, and not indirectly through the multitude of later writers who have borrowed from it, often without acknowledgement.

2 London *Economist*, Nov. 10, 1855, pp. 1129–30; Nov. 8, 1856, p. 1229. Tooke and Newmarch, V, 253; VI, 78–81, 197. Next to *A History of Prices*, the London *Economist* is the single most valuable source for the financial developments of the fifties.

The period from 1850 to 1857 was one of fluctuating prosperity and depression. Nevertheless, a general upswing in industrial activity in trade can be traced. The course of this economic movement was retarded or advanced by financial and banking crises and by several periods of poor harvests in various parts of Europe. The financial and banking difficulties arose from the influx of gold, the accelerated development of industry, transportation, and trade, and from political events.

The influence of political events from 1848 until 1857 is the simplest to describe and will serve as a general background for an account of the more complex economic developments. To a certain extent these political movements were themselves the products of economic conditions during the late 1840's. The last upheaval of the Chartists followed closely upon the failure of the Irish harvests and the severe but brief depression of 1847. In its turn, the revival of trade and the announcement of the California gold discoveries produced a new prosperity by 1850 which did much to hasten the rapid and unexpected demise of Chartism. The decline of the trade-union movement and the virtual cessation of organized demands of the poorer classes restored to the property owners, investors, and merchants much of the confidence which they had lost in 1847 in the persistence of customary social conditions.[3]

On the Continent the social upheaval was far more drastic and therefore far more effective in disrupting customary economic relationships. Hastened by the depression of 1847, the revolution of 1848 checked incipient manifestations of recovery and created a stagnation of economic life for the next two years.[4] The triumph of the counter-revolution, symbolized by the coup d'état of Napoleon III, ushered in what contemporary observers thought would be a new era of unrivaled prosperity. Although these prognostications were by no means correct, it is safe to say that the Second Empire created a political

[3] Exception should be made of the great strike at Preston in 1853–54. For an account of its causes and effects see Tooke and Newmarch, V, 294–97.

[4] Tooke and Newmarch, VI, 155 ff.

condition favorable to an upswing in the economic activity of the French middle class. The trade-union movement was rigorously suppressed, the liberal and radical clubs disbanded, and the powers of the state enlisted in the service of bankers and industrialists. That this prosperity failed to materialize in France was not due to any internal political disturbances, but rather to the external policy pursued by the government of Napoleon III and to economic developments beyond its control.

The Crimean War placed a strain upon the financial systems of the allies, borne without much immediate difficulty in England, but with great difficulty in France. In England the net addition to the public debt necessitated by the war was £32,371,495.[5] This sum was easily raised, and even the increases in taxation were but lightly felt. The shipments of specie to the Near East for the payment and support of the armed forces was a contributing factor to the continued stringency in the money market after 1854, as will be seen below. However, the war was fought in regions remote from the main routes of commerce and with an opponent who did not possess a navy capable of disrupting English trade. Although Russia was an important source of supply and market for England, this loss was easily overcome by the unprecedented expansion of English commerce with the United States during 1855 and 1856. It was rather the indirect effect of the Crimean War, reaching England through its connections with the Continent, which had the stronger influence upon the economic structure of that country.

On the other hand, France was directly and profoundly affected by the war. To the annual deficits, which had become almost habitual in France since the early years of the 1840's, was added the debt created by the war. Combined with the other factors which weakened the French financial structure, it produced the severe banking difficulties of 1856. Approxi-

[5] London *Economist*, May 17, 1856, pp. 529–30.

mately $300,000,000 was added to the public debt by the war, and large amounts of specie left the country for the Near East.[6] The contradictory effects of the expansion of credit and the contraction of specie shook the French financial system, already weakened by the speculative mania, poor harvests, and currency readjustments of the years from 1853 to 1856. At every stage the developing crisis in France reacted unfavorably upon the English situation and was, in the end, far more important than the direct effect of the Crimean War on the British Isles.

To a lesser extent, political events after 1848 reacted upon the economic life of the other European nations. Still largely dominated by an agricultural economy, they profited by poor harvests in England and France and were successful in attracting sums from English and French investors. It is true that minor monetary crises shook the banking systems of Holland, Germany, and Scandinavia, but until the depression of 1857 the effects were by no means disruptive to agriculture, commerce, and industry.[7]

Just as France was the political nerve center of Europe throughout the first half of the nineteenth century, so during the years from 1850 to 1857 it was the center from which fluctuations in the economic cycle radiated. This peculiar position arose not because France was economically dominant or strategically placed within international trade or finance. On the contrary, it was the very weakness of French economic life which made France so important in the world economic picture. These weaknesses were in turn derived from the basic transformation which France was experiencing during the mid years of the century. An analysis of French commerce and finance from 1850 to 1857 will make this clear.

After the consolidation of its power at the end of 1851, the

[6] See below, p. 44.

[7] *Parliamentary Papers*, 1857–58, V, 177. London *Economist*, Oct. 18, 1856, p. 1150.

government of Louis Napoleon was able to turn its attention to the economic rehabilitation of France. The interest of the landed proprietors and the great bankers, the groups most influential under the preceding monarchies, were subordinated to those of the industrialists and entrepreneurs. The internal policy of the French government during the decade of the 1850's was primarily designated to benefit these two groups.

The basic desire of the French industrialists and promoters was to prevent a repetition of the "June Days," when the whole structure of society had been threatened from below. In order to remove the threat of social revolution, the government adopted a twofold policy. On the one hand, the trade unions and liberal and radical groups were rigorously suppressed. On the other, an extensive system of social legislation was promulgated in an effort to remove the causes for popular discontent. Chief among these schemes was a financial institution created by the state—the *Caisse de la Boulangerie,* or Baker's Bank.

The *Caisse de la Boulangerie* was established in Paris by imperial decree in December, 1853, and during the course of the next year similar institutions were set up in other large centers of population throughout the country. The purpose of the *Caisse* was to sell bread to the poor below the market during years of scarcity when prices were high. Losses entailed by this practice would be met by the issuance of municipal bonds. In theory these bonds would eventually be redeemed by means of the profits made during years of plenty and low prices, when bread would be sold by the *Caisse* above the market. In order to put this scheme into effect, the *Caisse* was granted a monopoly of the sale of flour, and all bakers were under its control. The *Caisse* fixed the price at which bread might be sold by the bakers. The intention of the *Caisse* and of the government was to maintain a uniform price for bread, regardless of the fluctuations in the price of wheat, in the hope that profits and losses would not only average themselves out but would also absorb interest charges and cost of management.

Regardless of the theoretical defects of the plan, it was doomed to failure in practice by the unfavorable harvests of 1853 and 1854. In June, 1856, the debt of the *Caisse* was estimated at almost $10,000,000. Two successive increases in the price of bread were authorized by the government, but the losses of the *Caisse* continued to mount. Nor did a gratuity from the government of almost $5,000,000 do more than check for a time the growing insolvency of the institution. The experiences of the Parisian *Caisse* were duplicated in other large cities.[8]

During these same years a gigantic public works program was undertaken. While it provided work for the unemployed, it profited those industries and contractors who supplied the materials and undertook the construction. It was as part of this program that Baron Huysmans began his reconstruction of Paris, cutting straight boulevards through the city and eliminating the medieval maze of streets in which barricades were so easily raised. Almost $125,000,000 was spent by the state on public works during the years 1852–56 inclusive. This sum was approximately equal to the deficits of the French budget during the same period. In addition, the municipalities and departments of France spent vast sums on public improvements, estimated at more than $300,000,000 by 1856.[9]

Paralleling the construction of public works by the state was a gigantic railroad building program undertaken largely with private capital, both native and foreign. From 1852 to 1856 inclusive almost $350,000,000 was invested in railroads, only $25,000,000 of which was governmental funds. This figure is in marked contrast to the expenditure of the preceding twenty-two years, when less than $275,000,000 was spent on railroads. By the end of 1856 there were 4,036 miles of railway

[8] Tooke and Newmarch, VI, 28–32.

[9] Émile de Laveleye, *Le Marché monétaire et ses crises depuis cinquante ans*, Paris, 1865, p. 40. Tooke and Newmarch, VI, 19, 25–27, 660.

in operation. Although the mileage of French railroads was two fifths that of the English and only one sixth that of American railroads, it nevertheless represented a sizable achievement, considering the lateness of France's entrance into this field of construction. Concessions to build railroads were granted with a lavish hand by Louis Napoleon on terms far more beneficial to the proprietors than anything done by the Orléans monarchy. With construction costs averaging about $150,000 per mile, it is easy to understand why French railroad concessions were so popular among entrepreneurs in France and in England.[10]

To assist in the financing of these ambitious projects, the government granted amazingly generous charters to finance companies of all sorts. Chief among these was the *Crédit Mobilier*. Under the name of the *Société Générale de Crédit Mobilier*, there was established by imperial decree in November, 1852, a joint-stock company with a capital of 600,000,000 francs. The powers of the *Crédit Mobilier* were extremely broad. It could issue bonds, backed by holdings of securities, in amounts equal to ten times its capital; it could receive deposits, make loans, underwrite flotations of stocks and bonds, and manage companies in which it possessed an interest; it could promote all types of industrial and commercial enterprises at home and abroad.

This amazing finance company, which its promoters predicted would usher in a new era of perpetual prosperity, seemed successful from the start. Its shares sold at a premium before the company began operations and were popular in England as well as in France. The *Crédit Mobilier* plunged immediately into promotions of all kinds, especially railways and steamship lines, not only in France, but also in Spain, Austria, and Germany. Dividends of 10 percent and 13 percent were paid in 1853 and 1854. But by 1855 the company was deeply involved in stock market speculations, in an effort

[10] Laveleye, p. 40. Tooke and Newmarch, V, 379–83; VI, 32–39.

to sustain the price of securities which it owned and against which it had issued substantial amounts of its own obligations. Under the circumstances, a bold face had to be put on, and in 1855 the *Crédit Mobilier* paid a dividend of almost 50 percent, much of it out of capital. During 1856 and the first half of 1857 the shares of the company steadily declined, not only because of its own precarious condition but also because the entire credit structure of France was involved in increasing difficulties.[11]

An early rival of the *Crédit Mobilier* and one of its ultimate successors was the *Crédit Foncier.* Founded by imperial decree in February, 1852, and in July, 1854, given a status similar to that of the Bank of France, the *Crédit Foncier* was a joint-stock corporation which could make loans on real estate throughout France and issue securities equal in value to the loans which it made. It was hoped that the *Crédit Foncier* would materially reduce the rate of interest on mortgages, which during the 1840's averaged about 7 percent. At first the *Crédit Foncier* charged 5 percent for its loans, but eventually was forced to raise its rate to almost 6 percent. The obligations of the institution were issued in amounts ranging from 1,000 francs to 10 francs, and interest at 3 percent was paid on them through an elaborate lottery system. As a result the low-priced obligations of the *Crédit Foncier* were extremely popular because of the gambling element involved. By the end of 1855 the outstanding liabilities of the *Crédit Foncier* were about $20,000,000. In chartering the *Crédit Foncier* the government of Napoleon III was moved by two motives—to increase the credit facilities available to the owners of landed property and to reduce the rate of interest generally. In neither of these aims was the *Crédit Foncier* particularly successful. The amount of its loans on landed property averaged only $13,-

[11] L. H. Jenks, *The Migration of British Capital to 1875*, New York, 1927, pp. 240–45. Tooke and Newmarch, VI, 104–21. See also an interesting article on the activities of the *Crédit Mobilier* by the Paris correspondent of the New York *Tribune*, July 27, 1857.

000,000 by 1856, and, as noted above, its interest rate was raised to approximately 6 percent within a short period.[12]

The reduction of the rate of interest was a prime concern pf the French government and naturally of the large group of promoters and industrialists for whom the government was to solicitous. A reduction in the rate of interest was bound to nave a stimulating effect upon the promotion of railroads, steamship lines, factory construction, and other enterprises. As long as money rates were correspondingly low across the Channel, a decrease in the interest rates in France would not necessarily result in a drain of gold, especially if the profits of industrial and railroad promotions were large. With these considerations in mind, the French government in March, 1852, reduced the rate of interest on the 5 percent *rentes* to 4½ percent. It was hoped that the conversion of almost $500,000,000 worth of government obligations from 5 to 4½ percent would powerfully influence the rate of interest in France. The conversion was attended by considerable difficulties, and it was finally necessary for the government to reimburse the losses of the bankers who underwrote the new loan by issuing to them an equivalent amount of *rentes* bearing 3 percent interest. As a result the treasury was by no means a gainer nor was the rate of interest seriously affected. Nevertheless, the whole transaction bears witness to the desire of the government to stimulate expansion by encouraging low interest rates.[13]

Far more important than this conversion of the 5 percent *rentes* was the reduction in March, 1852, in the Bank of France rate from 4 percent to 3 percent, largely as a result of government pressure. This reduction was accompanied by an amendment to the bank's charter which permitted that institution to lend money to railroads. As a concession, the charter of the bank, which was to terminate in 1855, was extended

[12] Tooke and Newmarch, VI, 92–99. Jenks, p. 245.
[13] Tooke and Newmarch, VI, 20–24.

until 1867. For over a year the bank was able to maintain a rate without precedent in its previous history, but by October, 1853, the loss of specie compelled an increase to 5 percent. It was quite obvious that the financial situation of the country did not permit the maintenance of a 3-percent rate for very long, despite the fact that during the same period the Bank of England was charging a like premium for its discounts.[14]

The speculative boom of 1853 and 1854 went on, despite the fact that the French agricultural situation was becoming increasingly bad. Poor harvests began as early as 1852, but each year was successively worse until the end of 1856. During these years France was forced to import grain from abroad, chiefly from the United States. As was seen above in connection with the *Caisse de la Boulangerie,* grain prices rose higher and higher until by 1855 they were double what they had been in 1850, a year of ample harvest. Added to the poor harvests of grain, the silk crop was below the average in 1855 and failed in 1856. This, in turn, necessitated large imports of a raw material ordinarily produced in sufficient quantities in France.[15]

It was against such a background that the French government undertook in 1854 to raise the money necessary for carrying on the Crimean War. Naturally the Crimean War loans took on the same speculative character as most of the outstanding financial transactions of the period. The French government borrowed almost $300,000,000 during 1854 and 1855. Considering the liberal terms offered and the quantity of credit existing in the country, it was no wonder that the loan was oversubscribed four times. Because of its low interest policy, the French government paid no more than 3 and 4½ percent on the loans, but compensated for this by offering liberal

[14] Tooke and Newmarch, VI, 65–71.

[15] Alphonse Courtois, *Histoire de la Banque de France,* Paris, 1875, p. 228. Gabriel Ramon, *Histoire de la Banque de France,* Paris, 1929, pp. 260–63. Clément Juglar, *Les Crises commerciales et leur retour périodique,* Paris, 1889, pp. 270–74. Laveleye, pp. 118–19, 245–46. Tooke and Newmarch, V, 34–37.

discounts for cash payments and by permitting installment buying to be spread over fifteen months without loss of interest on unpaid installments.[16] Despite the initial success of the loans, their net effect was to aggravate the already-existing instability of French economic conditions, for almost two thirds of the proceeds was shipped in the form of specie to the Near East for the purpose of paying and supplying the troops. So severe a drain of specie, combined with the already existing drain arising from the poor harvests and the unfavorable balance of trade with the Far East, created a series of banking crises which steadily weakened the inflated credit structure of France. An analysis of these banking crises will be given with the following account of English economic development from 1850 to 1856.

During the same years that France was experiencing simultaneously the economic extremes of overspeculation and poor harvests, England's development was on the whole more prosperous. The brightest feature in the English picture was the unprecedented growth of over-sea commerce. The following table gives the overall figures for this growth from 1851 through 1855: [17]

Year	*Imports*	*Exports*
1851		£ 89,600,000
1852		93,100,000
1853		117,500,000
1854	£152,500,000	115,700,000
1855	143,600,000	116,600,000

The invisible items in the trade balance—freight charges, insurance charges, export of capital, profits, and so forth—were sufficiently large to provide a net balance in favor of England.

This favorable development of trade, however, was not without its temporary setbacks. For one thing, agricultural

16 André Liesse, *Evolution of Credit and Banks in France*, Washington, 1909, p. 87. Courtois, p. 218. Tooke and Newmarch, VI, 661–67.

17 The import figures for 1851–53 are still given in the antiquated "official value" form and are comparatively worthless. *Parliamentary Papers*, 1856, LX, 271 ff.

conditions were not good. The below-average harvest of 1852 and the very poor harvest of 1853 necessitated heavy importations of foreign grain. During the winter of 1853–54 more grain was imported from abroad than during the disastrous years of the famine of the 1840's. That these increased importations were not due to the repeal of the Corn Laws may be seen from the fact that prices were highest during the period from 1852 to 1854, when the bulk of the importations occurred. During the winter of 1854–55 prices were as high again, yet only half as many goods were imported.[18]

The failure of the harvest in 1853 and the first gathering clouds of the approaching war with Russia brought a halt to the upward expansion of commerce and industry. Throughout the winter of 1853–54 business marked time, but by the summer American demand was sufficient to lift it out of the doldrums.[19] The Crimean War had remarkably little effect upon English commerce. Normal channels were not disturbed, and raw materials ordinarily obtained in Russia were procured elsewhere, especially in India and China.[20] Nor did the war have much effect upon the steady growth of the British railroad system. From the beginning of 1851 until the end of 1856 over $300,000,000 was invested in railroad construction within the British Isles.[21]

Except for poor harvests, the picture of both English and French development thus far presented is one of steadily increasing prosperity. And so, in the main, it was. The prime mover of this prosperity was the new gold of California and Australia. But by 1855 the expansion of trade and credit was too great for the sustaining power of the specie reserves of England and France, under existing methods of international and intranational payments. Speculation overtaxed the abilities of monetary circulations and of banking systems based

18 Tooke and Newmarch, Vol. V, Part I, *passim*.
19 Tooke and Newmarch, V, 284–307.
20 London *Economist*, Aug. 8, 1857, p. 869.
21 Tooke and Newmarch, V, 351–55, 379–83.

upon specie. The discrepancy between the means of payment and the quantity of payments which had to be made brought about the collapse of the boom.

This discrepancy appeared first in European and above all in English relationships with the Near, Middle, and Far East. With all these regions western Europe had an unfavorable balance of trade which was greatly aggravated during the four years from 1854 to 1857 by a series of special circumstances—the Crimean War, the export of capital to India, the Chinese and Persian wars of 1856–57, and the Indian Mutiny. Each of these will be outlined in turn.

The effect of the Crimean War was twofold. Large quantities of specie were shipped to the Near East by England and France for paying and equipping their forces in the theaters of operations. France was estimated to have sent almost $200,000,000, and England could not have sent much less for this purpose.[22] The second effect of the Crimean War was to increase the importance of India and China as sources of raw materials previously obtained from Russia or needed in larger quantities because of the war.[23] Contributing to the growth of Indian and Chinese exports was the failure of the French silk harvest in 1855 and 1856 and of the Italian harvest in 1857.[24] American consumption of tea rose during the prosperous years of the mid 1850's. At the same time civil wars in China reduced the ability of that country to absorb European or Indian products.[25] The net result was a balance of trade which favored India and China most heavily. Under normal conditions this unfavorable balance was usually absorbed by the "invisible items" accruing to the benefit of England. Regardless of the destination of Indian and Chinese exports, the financing of this commerce and the transportation

[22] Ramon, p. 260.
[23] See above, n. 20. Also London *Economist*, Aug. 1, 1857, p. 839; Sept. 17, 1859, p. 1035.
[24] See above, n. 15.
[25] Tooke and Newmarch, VI, 679.

of most of it was in English hands.[26] But from 1855 to 1857 the "invisible items" were insufficient to balance the export of goods from the Far East because of the growth of British capital investments in India.

Tooke and Newmarch estimated that from 1851 to 1857 more than £14,000,000 was subscribed in London for the construction of Indian railways, at least half of which was actually remitted to India.[27] Because the annual tribute exacted from India and the "invisible items" in the trade balance served only to equalize the export of goods from India to the rest of the world, capital investment in India could be effected only by a shipment of specie, principally silver. From 1851 to 1859 inclusive more than $200,000,000 in specie was shipped from Europe to the Far East, of which $175,000,000 was silver. Over $70,000,000 in silver went to the Far East through England in the single year 1856, and the total for 1857 was close to $100,000,000.[28]

Nor was India alone the recipient of capital exports. From the end of the Crimean War dated the beginning of that interest in Near Eastern investments which was to reach its peak during the 1870's. In the six months from January, 1856, to July, 1856, twenty-two companies with capital totaling $100,000,000 were formed to build railroads, industrial enterprises, and harbor works in the Near East, South America, and the Balkans. The entire capital for the construction of the Suez Canal was raised in France, beginning in 1856. No reliable estimates are obtainable of the actual export of capital to the Near East prior to the fall of 1857.[29]

The year 1857 witnessed increasing exports of specie to India and China, largely for commercial and political reasons.

[26] Tooke and Newmarch, Vol. VI, Appendix XXIII, *passim.*

[27] Tooke and Newmarch, VI, 716–17. See also Jenks, p. 213.

[28] Tooke and Newmarch, Vol. VI, Appendix XXIII, *passim.* London *Economist,* Nov. 10, 1855, pp. 1129–30; Nov. 8, 1856, pp. 1229–30; Sept. 19, 1857, p. 1033; Oct. 24, 1857, p. 1178. Laveleye, pp. 51 n., 118–19, 240, 245–46.

[29] London *Economist,* July 5, 1856, p. 726. Jenks, pp. 168, 297–98, 300–5.

Chief among the latter were the demands made upon English resources for the Chinese and Persian wars fought during the winter of 1856–57. By the spring of 1857 the East India Company was in serious straits, as a result of these additional expenses. It needed only the news of the outbreak of the Mutiny to bring about a general realization that exports of specie to India would undoubtedly be far greater than anything experienced hitherto.[30]

The factor most important in determining the causes of the crisis of 1857 is the source of the specie exported to the Near East and to India and China from the spring of 1854 to the summer of 1857. During this period probably $700,000,000 in specie was shipped to the Near and Far East.[31] Much of the specie shipped to the Near East during the Crimean War returned to England and France within a relatively short period through the normal operations of commerce. Specie sent to India and China, however, was totally lost to the European economy.

During the early 1850's a number of changes in European monetary systems occurred which offer one clue to the source of much of the silver which found its way to Asia. Holland, Belgium, Hamburg and other states of Germany went on a silver standard during the early 1850's. Silver was therefore readily obtainable in these regions. The banks of Holland and Hamburg were able to retain their precious reserves only by charging high rates of discount and by obtaining "accommodation" credits on London, which they used for the repurchase of their lost silver.[32]

But by far the greatest source of silver supply was France, where silver had been virtually demonetized early in the 1850's. Coinage of silver was practically discontinued after 1852, while coinage of gold rose to unprecedented proportions. During the period from 1852 to 1857 inclusive the net loss of

[30] London *Economist*, Oct. 10, 1857, pp. 1117–18. [31] See n. 28.
[32] See n. 2; London *Economist*, Oct. 18, 1856, p. 1150; Laveleye, pp. 49, 91–92.

silver by France was in excess of $250,000,000. During the same years, however, the net gain of gold was almost $350,000,000. The net gain in specie was probably less than $100,000,000, all of this in gold.[33] This sum was far too small to serve as a basis for the tremendous expansion of commerce, industry, and speculation which occurred during the 1850's. This was especially true in view of the fact that payments within France were made almost exclusively in coin and not by means of paper.[34] The net accretion to French specie stocks of $100,000,000 was all made into coin, and in addition quantities of plate and bullion were sent to the mint in order to provide for the growing needs of the metallic circulation.[35] From the beginning of 1855 until the end of 1857 French banks, and especially the Bank of France, had the utmost difficulty in maintaining specie reserves. An account of the expedients resorted to by the Bank of France will make clear the nature of the incipient financial crisis facing France during these three years.

As has been shown above, the desire of the French government for a low interest rate brought about a reduction of the Bank of France rate to 3 percent during 1852 and most of 1853. By October, 1853, the specie reserves had fallen from $120,000,000 to $75,000,000, while discounts had risen by $50,000,000. Accordingly the Bank of France rate was raised to 4 percent and in January, 1854, to 5 percent, after a further reduction of $15,000,000 in the specie reserve. By May, 1854, the bullion had risen to $80,000,000, and the discount rate was reduced to 4 percent. As the pressure became greater during 1855 the bank tried desperately to avert an increase in its rate, but was finally forced to yield. In October, 1855, the money rate was advanced to 5 percent and then to 6 percent, the legal maximum, while the length of bills was reduced from 90 to 75 days. At this time the specie reserves of the

[33] Laveleye, p. 250. London *Economist*, Oct. 25, 1856, p. 175.
[34] Tooke and Newmarch, VI, 55. [35] Tooke and Newmarch, VI, 154–55.

Bank of France were only $45,000,000, while the discounts had risen to almost $100,000,000. A temporary easing of the situation at the close of the Crimean War brought the rate down to 5 percent in March, 1856, but by September the legal maximum of 6 percent was once again reached and the length of bills was reduced to 60 days. Specie reserves were a little over $30,000,000, while discounts had risen to $110,000,000. The inflation of credit, as represented by the discounts, had increased at a greater rate than the decline in the specie reserves.[36]

The loss of specie by the Bank of France, amounting to $90,000,000 from 1852 to the end of 1856, was actually more than double this amount. From July, 1855, until December, 1856, the bank purchased $135,000,000 worth of gold in London at a premium of over $2,000,000.[37] The total net loss of the Bank of France was therefore $220,000,000, the specie reserve being $35,000,000 in December, 1856.

These extraordinary purchases in London were made in the most devious manner by the Bank of France so as not to attract attention to either its plight or its practices. The house of Rothschild, with its wide connections in the money markets of the world, was employed by the bank to purchase quantities of English bills on the Continent, present them for payment when due or discount them, demand the proceeds in Bank of England notes, and offer the notes for redemption in gold at the Bank of England. The specie was then shipped to France and purchased from the Rothschilds and their agents by the Bank of France. Naturally the premiums and profits of these transactions remained with the Rothschilds.[38]

Although each new purchase temporarily eased the situation of the Bank of France, it provided no permanent relief for a number of reasons. While the circulation of the Bank of

[36] Tooke and Newmarch, VI, 638–52. [37] Tooke and Newmarch, VI, 87n.

[38] Tooke and Newmarch, VI, 85–91; Pierre Dupont-Ferrier, *Le Marché financier de Paris sous le Second Empire,* Paris, 1925, pp. 28, 60. Ramon, pp. 260, 264–67, 270–71. Liesse, p. 88. London *Economist,* Oct. 22, 1855, p. 1146.

France notes decreased from January, 1853, to December, 1856, by $20,000,000, the metallic circulation increased by $100,000,000. This growth in the metallic circulation directly absorbed part of the specie lost by the Bank of France. The remainder of the specie lost by the bank also went into the metallic circulation but did not bring about an overall increase. It served to replace with gold coins the exact quantity of French silver coins which were drawn away, first to England and eventually to the Far East. The quantity and value of the metallic circulation were thus preserved and increased during these years at the expense of the specie reserves of the Bank of France.

The "Old Lady of Threadneedle Street" was not oblivious to the manner in which she was being plundered by her French counterpart.[39] Nor was the Bank of England able to stand this drain of its gold reserves without serious damage.

In the absence of exact estimates, the consensus of opinion seems to be that the net imports of new gold to England from 1851 to 1856 were between $500,000,000 and $550,000,000. Exports of gold during the same period were probably about $300,000,000. On the other hand, new silver imported totaled $150,000,000, while exports of silver were probably $250,000,000. Since the import figures in both cases included only specie coming from countries producing precious metals, it is safe to say that at a minimum the net gain of gold was at least $250,000,000 and the net loss of silver was at least $100,000,000.[40] Gold coinage, added to the metallic circulation and paid out through the Bank of England during the period from 1852 through 1856, was almost $200,000,000.[41] This meant an apparent deficit in England's specie holdings of approximately $50,000,000, an amount which was amply covered by the imports of specie from regions which were not producers of the precious metals—France, Germany, Italy, and the Levant.

[39] London *Economist*, Oct. 13, 1855, p. 1118.
[40] *Parliamentary Papers*, 1861, LXII, 46. Laveleye, p. 249.
[41] Tooke and Newmarch, VI, 538–58.

However, the experience of the Bank of England shows that the net increase in the specie holdings of England was by no means large enough to strengthen the position of the English banks during the years of expanding trade and speculation. Above all, the increase was insufficient to enable the Bank of England to stand the raid upon its gold reserves carried out by the Bank of France.

From April, 1852, until January, 1853, the Bank of England rate was only 2 percent. During this period the bullion fell from the unprecedented high of $110,000,000 to $95,000,000, while discounts rose from $50,000,000 to almost $75,000,000. In January, 1853, the discount rate was raised to 3 percent and in September to 5 percent, when specie reserves sank to $75,000,000. By May, 1854, the specie holdings fell to $60,000,000 and the rate was raised to 5½ percent. The discount rate fluctuated between 4 percent and 5 percent until October, 1855, when discounts rose to $90,000,000 and specie fell to $55,000,000. The rate was then raised to 7 percent. By November, 1856, the specie was down to less than $45,000,000, while discounts had risen still further to $100,000,000. During the winter of 1856–57 and until the outbreak of the panic in October, 1857, the Bank of England rate fluctuated between 6 percent and 7 percent because the state of specie reserves continued very grave. Throughout this whole period the circulation of the Bank of England notes fell from a high of $120,000,000 in 1853 to a low of $95,000,000 in 1856.[41]

This inability of the Bank of England to maintain its specie reserves was in large part caused by the gold-buying practices of the Bank of France. The Bank of France bought $135,000,000 worth of gold in England from July, 1855, until December, 1856. During this period the Bank of England lost half of its gold, or $45,000,000. Nor was it able to check this loss, because at least $90,000,000 of the new gold reaching England was drained away to France as fast as it entered the Bank of England. The only consolation was the knowledge that the

Bank of France was having even greater difficulties in maintaining its specie reserves and that its losses were much larger. Nor should it be forgotten that while the Bank of France was buying England's gold at a premium, England was carrying away far greater quantities of French silver for shipment to India and China.

The net effect of the drain of specie from the Bank of England was to force the bank's discount rate up to 7 percent and the London money market rate for first-class bills up to 8 percent.[42] Thus the gold of California and Australia, which was supposed to usher in the era of cheap money, actually brought about the highest rates which the century had yet experienced, exclusive of crisis years.

The prevalence in England of high money rates from the fall of 1855 until the summer of 1857 had a disastrous effect upon American security values. There was little incentive for the English to invest in highly speculative American stocks and bonds paying 7 percent when prime short-term paper paying 8 percent was readily obtainable at home.[43] In the face of this basic economic advantage, English investors hardly needed the experiences of the Schuyler frauds and the railroad rate wars to convince them that their money was both safer and more remunerative when invested in England and France. Even Indian railway bonds, on which at least 5 percent interest was guaranteed by the East India Company, were preferable to American ones.[44]

Every increase in the Bank of England rate brought renewed liquidation of British investments in American securities. Nor was the American market able to absorb this prolonged selling without serious losses. The prices of American stocks and bonds, principally railroads, declined steadily throughout 1856 and 1857. With the decline in security values

[42] Tooke and Newmarch, VI, 557.

[43] See the lament of the *Bankers' Magazine*, Nov., 1856, p. 414.

[44] Nalinaksha Sanyal, *Development of Indian Railways*, Calcutta, 1930, Chapter II, *passim*.

there vanished a large part of the assets which supported American banks, financial houses, and insurance companies. As a consequence, an economic crisis of major proportions occurred in the United States, as we shall see in the next chapter.

CHAPTER FOUR

THE CRISIS OF 1857 IN THE UNITED STATES

THE CONDITIONS set forth in the preceding chapter were soon reflected in the economic life of the United States. By June, 1857, the amount of indebtedness incurred by railways, manufacturers, and promoters of all kinds to the banks of the country and to each other had so far overreached the saturation point that the New York *Herald* inquired despairingly:

What can be the end of all this but another general collapse like that of 1837, only upon a much grander scale? The same premonitory symptoms that prevailed in 1835–6 prevail in 1857 in a tenfold degree. Government spoliations, public defaulters, paper bubbles of all descriptions, a general scramble for western lands and town and city sites, millions of dollars, made or borrowed, expended in fine houses and gaudy furniture; hundreds of thousands in the silly rivalries of fashionable parvenues, in silks, laces, diamonds and every variety of costly frippery are only a few among the many crying evils of the day. The worst of all these evils is the moral pestilence of luxurious exemption from honest labor, which is infecting all classes of society. The country merchant is becoming a city stockjobber, and the honest country farmer has gone off among the gamblers in western land. Thus, as this general scramble among all classes to be rich at once, and by the shortest possible cut, extends and increases, our rogues, defaulters and forgers are multiplied. The epidemic and its attending evils must run their course.[1]

The *Herald* was by no means alone in predicting a collapse, for other newspapers and periodicals throughout the nation sounded frequent alarms well in advance of the crisis. While

[1] New York *Herald,* June 27, 1857.

money continued plentiful, however, public psychology had little patience with such pessimism; and money did continue fairly plentiful in certain sections through July, 1857.[2]

There had been, indeed, a definite recession in certain industries following the close of the Crimean War, as we have noted. The farmer suffered from the reopening of the Russian grain trade, which caused a decrease in the demand for breadstuffs for export. Shipping interests, too, were rather seriously affected by the loss of this trade. But the public generally continued to prosper. As late as February, 1857, the *Herald,* which on earlier occasions had written along contrary lines, cited its own increased circulation to more than 80,000 copies daily as evidence of "the dawning of exceedingly brisk and prosperous times." In view of the promotional nature of the announcement, it must be discounted to some degree, yet its very extravagance is simple proof that prosperity was still predominantly the order of the day. "Indeed," said the *Herald,* "there is every indication through all of the walks of life that the great commercial and financial epoch now opening will, for the next three years, be one of unparalleled prosperity, credit, extravagance and speculation, and that our commercial and business operations of this spring, of all kinds, will immensely exceed the operations of the spring trade of any previous year in our history." [3]

That the prediction fell considerably short of realization may be gathered from the following report on the spring trade, written in July:

> The usual June dullness has prevailed during the month, and trade has been very quiet at the centers of business in all parts of the country. The course of the spring trade has been such as to create considerable uneasiness in regard to the future, but this arises more from uncertainty than from any positive indications of future trouble. . . . The question in regard to the approaching season turns upon the recuperative power of the West. The speculative fever in that section appears to have reached its height.

[2] *Bankers' Magazine,* II, 750.

[3] New York *Herald,* Feb. 5, 1857.

Everyone who had anything to invest has "taken a turn" in real estate, and many have made large fortunes by the advance in town and city lots, and in farms contiguous to new railroad stations; but money is scarce and very dear, and those who now hold the property may find it difficult either to pay for it, or to sell it without great loss.[4]

During July the conviction grew among the more sober and critical citizenry in all sections of the country that "the great commercial and financial epoch" was not going to last another three years. Instead of the spring trade "immensely exceeding that of any previous year in history," the *Herald* reported on July 18 that imports had fallen off during the spring from 20 to 50 percent and that receipts of the two great railroads carrying the bulk of traffic between New York and the West, namely, the Erie and the New York Central, had fallen off in the aggregate $220,000 in the month of June as compared with June, 1856.

Prices of all commodities, however, remained high and the general cost of living was fully 40 percent greater than it had been four years earlier. Not only had there been an unwarranted rise in sugar and cotton prices, but virtually all raw materials used in manufacture had been similarly inflated. With the business decline of the spring, therefore, manufacturers began to find themselves unable to continue operations at a profit. In July the Stark Mills in Manchester, N.H., which annually consumed 15,000 bales of cotton, suspended entirely, declaring it impossible to market their goods without a loss, despite the fact that they had in their warehouses a four-month supply of raw cotton which they had purchased at a time when prices were three cents lower. Because their goods had accumulated alarmingly, they considered it wiser to stop manufacturing and lose the interest on the raw material than to go on and add to the dead capital the additional cost of labor.[5]

[4] *Hunt's Merchants' Magazine*, XXXVII, 70.
[5] New York *Herald*, July 18, 1857.

Another large mill in Rockport, Maine, announced at about the same time that it had stopped manufacturing because of an unusual surplus of goods on hand and the impossibility of selling them at remunerative prices. With markets full and the demand light, the largest mills in Lowell, Mass., likewise curtailed their operations. Some reduced their running to a four-day week, while others announced they were "stopping for repairs, which are not likely to be completed before November," meaning in plain language that they were stopping the useless manufacture of goods until the people could buy them.[6]

Said the *Herald:* "The ability of the mass of families to buy new clothing this year is not so great as heretofore, and economy and severe retrenchment from all but necessaries is the universal rule. That a storm is brewing on the commercial horizon there can be no doubt. He who runs may read." [7]

The weekly tables of the New York Clearing House Association for 1857, however, give clear indication that the New York banks did not attach immediate significance to the slump. During the four-week period between July 4 and August 1 the banks increased their loans by $5,500,000 to the aggregate of $120,597,050, while their deposits expanded by $3,500,000 to $68,682,088. Specie and circulation remained fairly static at $12,918,014 and $8,665,422 respectively.

In the following week, despite a reduction of more than $1,000,000 in both specie and deposits, the banks continued extending credit until they had raised their total loans to the unprecedented high point of $122,077,252. It was a point that was not to be touched again for many months to come.

Before attaching too much significance to August 8 as a turning point, however, it is well to take note of Gibbons' observations on this subject.[8] He turns back to the Clearing

[6] *Ibid.* [7] *Ibid.*

[8] James Sloan Gibbons, author of *The Banks of New York, Their Dealers, the Clearing House, and the Panic of 1857* (New York, 1858), has written one of the best contemporary accounts of the causes and effects of the panic.

House records of the four preceding years and points out what is indeed a remarkable parallelism of movement. In every case the month of August saw the attainment of the year's peak in bank loans. In the years 1853, 1854, and 1856 loans reached their highest level in the first week of August; in 1855, in the third week of August, and in 1857, in the second week of August. They began to fall on these dates and reached their lowest ebb in the second week of November in 1853, 1856, and 1857; in the third week of November in 1855, and in the second week of December in 1854. There is a general concurrence of movement in respect to loans, deposits, and specie. The year 1857 is exceptional, therefore, only in respect to the violence of fluctuation after August.[9]

Reduced to round numbers, the Clearing House report on the condition of New York banks for the first three weeks of August, 1857, is as follows:

Week Ending:	*Loans*	*Specie*	*Circulation*	*Deposits*
August 8	$122,077,000	$11,737,000	$8,982,000	$67,372,000
August 15	121,241,000	11,361,000	8,780,000	66,815,000
August 22	120,140,000	10,097,000	8,694,000	64,241,000

The contraction here indicated follows the gradual scale of former years. In it we can perceive no particular disturbance of the commercial scene, no evidence of extraordinary apprehension.

On the morning of August 24, however, the highly respected Charles Stetson, president of the New York branch of the Ohio Life Insurance and Trust Company, made the following announcement, which, despite the seriousness of its implications, could hardly have been expected to produce so drastic an effect on the nation's commercial stability as it did:

The unpleasant duty has devolved upon me to state that this company has suspended payment. This event has mainly been brought about in consequence of making loans here to parties who are unable to respond at this time. I would add that the capital of the

[9] Gibbons, *op. cit.*, p. 337.

company, two millions, is sound and reliable, exclusive of such loss as may arise from insufficiency of securities pledged for loans above referred to.[10]

The general circumstances of the failure were not in themselves very alarming. The home office in Cincinnati was reported by telegraph to have its doors open as usual, with its affairs apparently unembarrassed, notwithstanding the plight of the New York branch. Further inquiry on the part of the press and the banking interests, however, brought to light the distressing fact that the entire assets of the institution had been virtually embezzled by its cashier under what were supposed to have been the watchful eyes of its officers and trustees.[11]

That such conditions could have existed in an institution such as the Ohio Life was almost unbelievable. For many years no banking institution in New York had enjoyed a more enviable reputation. None was favored with more deposits and none was abler to loan on adequate security. It does not appear that the Ohio Life ever did any insurance business, but as a bank of deposit with a capitalization of $2,000,000, it made loans in large volume. It was the depository of large sums from private individuals, who used it as a savings bank, and likewise from brokers, who put up their margins in its hands and drew a small interest thereon. It became the transfer agent of the state of Ohio and of various corporations within that state. It paid the state coupons. It advanced money to, and borrowed from, the state bank. In short, it was the nursing mother to all the financial institutions of Ohio.

On the day after the New York branch closed its doors it became known that the company's liabilities, of which the fifty-five New York banks held a major part, would total at least $5,000,000. The effect upon the Street was an immediate decline in stocks of from 3 to 7 percent.[12]

10 *Bankers' Magazine*, XII, 240.

11 *Hunt's Merchants' Magazine*, XXXVII, 462.

12 *Ibid.*

Public apprehension, generally speaking, was as nothing compared with the apprehension exhibited by the officers of the various New York banks. To them the Ohio Life's failure was an incident of blackest portent. This is apparent from the zeal with which they set about reducing their engagements, as though they had suddenly become aware of the dangers to which the whole financial system was exposed. If the Ohio Life's entire capital could be dissipated without discovery and even without arousing the suspicion of its own trustees, why might not similar frauds be concealed and propagated in other institutions of equally high repute? The question was still on their lips when news was received that the business house of John Thompson and Company, currently famed for the ease with which it had bought up the most recent state loan issue of $1,500,000, was completely wiped out in consequence of the Ohio Life's failure.[13]

Distrust spread like a malignant growth. No attempt was made by the New York banks, individually or collectively, to help the Ohio Life meet its obligations. If any such thought occurred to them it must have died a quick death for lack of anyone with the necessary combination of foresight and leadership. The desirability of preserving public confidence did not appear nearly so important to the bank managers as the expediency of fortifying the assets of their individual institutions. Disregarding its probable effect upon private enterprise, they entered upon a program of contraction which accomplished a $4,000,000-reduction of loans in less than a week.

Within forty-eight hours of the Ohio Life's failure the pressure of contraction was so strong that seven small banks in the rural sections of New York State, which depended upon the metropolitan banks for their existence, were forced to the wall. Within the metropolis itself, the public looked with

[13] The statistics and events chronicled below, for the next several pages, except where otherwise indicated, are in large part derived from the daily account of the critical period as found in *Panics and Revulsions in the United States*, by Members of the New York Press, 1857.

wonder and apprehension upon the stringent regulations the banks were collectively applying to all their transactions. Certification of checks was imposed with unaccustomed rigor, and the notes of houses in high standing were rejected when presented for payment unless the deposit to cover them was already made. Even the best dealers, who had never committed an impropriety, found that personal intercourse with the banks was extremely difficult. It was next to impossible to obtain even the most trivial accommodations without an exasperating series of delays and searching inquiries. Stocks held as collateral security were marked down in value from 10 to 30 percent, and successive installments on loans were required to restore the continuous depreciation caused by the process.

Coincident with the first week's reduction of bank loans from $120,000,000 to $116,000,000 were sporadic outbursts of alarm in the Stock Exchange, some of the leading issues registering losses of from two to five points in the course of a day's trading. Scarcity of money became an increasingly serious problem. As the second week of contraction began, many individuals and institutions that had relied on continued bank accommodations found themselves in severe straits. The Street resounded with wild rumors of approaching failures, rumors which by September 1 began to materialize with sickening regularity. The first day of the month witnessed a heavy toll of business houses unable to meet their engagements. The list included such reputable old institutions as the Mechanics' Banking Association; Beebee and Company, bullion dealers; and Adams and Buckingham. The situation was made no happier by the discovery that the teller of the Mechanics' Banking Association had contributed to that institution's demise by being personally in default to the amount of $72,000.

The report of the Clearing House Association on September 5 showed that its member banks had, for the second week in a row, reduced their total loans by $4,000,000. The news was not happily received. It merely served to emphasize the degree of pressure the banks were exerting upon the money market.

The situation was made the more critical by the fact that the banks, finding they could get back virtually none of the capital sunk in railroad ventures, were concentrating the entire force of their efforts upon recalling their capital from the more legitimate sources, to the ruination of many a worthy merchant and manufacturer. Consequently business houses, large and small, were finding themselves in constant need of liquidating their assets in order to escape the threat of insolvency. The stock market in its steady downward trend reflected the urgency of their efforts.

The ninth of September saw the failure of Fitshugh and Littlejohn, a large transportation company; the tenth was marked by numerous failures among dry-goods houses, and a decline of from three to five points in New York bank stocks. On the fourteenth Wesley and Company, stock brokers, suspended, and the Board of Brokers voted to restrict time sales to thirty days. The list of important failures grew alarmingly.

Then on the fifteenth, in the midst of news of extreme stringency in Philadelphia, Cincinnati, and Chicago, the newspapers revealed that the steamer "Central America," en route from Aspinwall (now Colon, Panama) to New York with $2,000,000 in gold aboard, was unreported and overdue. The market declined under feverish trading, and money went to unheard-of rates. On the seventeenth word was received that the "Central America" had gone down, a calamity which, aside from the heavy toll of human life, amounted to a total loss, including gold in hands of passengers and the value of the ship, of about $2,500,000. There was no insurance on the vessel, and only $500,000 of the gold had been covered. Excitement ran high, but the market stood the shock fairly well, declining only slightly during the next two days.

In this state of things, as Gibbons points out, the Clearing House daily settlements in specie exerted a crushing influence on the commercial interest and became a new source of terror. What in ordinary times was supposed to be a safeguard against unwise expansion of bank credits was now a remorseless power compelling the smaller banks—the majority of the whole—to a violent contraction of their loans to dealers, forcing the latter into the sacrifice of property and finally into bankruptcy. Not until weeks later, when the banks had been forced to suspend specie payments, did it occur to the managing committees of the Clearing House to relax this destructive rule and to permit the settlement of daily balances in United States or New York State bonds instead of in specie. By then the time had passed when it could be of material service to the merchant or manufacturer. Even so, it proved a wholesome alleviation for the banks themselves and went a long way toward preventing further depreciation and toward repairing the mischief that had been done.[14]

By the nineteenth of September bank loans had been reduced to $108,000,000, a contraction of $4,000,000 in two weeks. Announcement was made on the twenty-first of the failure of Persse and Brooks, and of Cyrus W. Field and Company, large paper dealers, while from Philadelphia came news of immense failures, including that of Caleb Cope and Company. There was intense pressure everywhere. In Philadelphia, the following day, public bewilderment crystallized into terror and resulted in a run on the banks. By September 25 the situation in Philadelphia was so acute that the banks of that city were forced into partial suspension of specie payments, and on the next day suspension was made complete. All eyes were turned to the New York banks in anticipation of a similar move. The stock market dropped sharply. Erie Railroad declined to 15; Reading to 37, a loss of 10 points in less than two weeks; Panama to 78, a 3-point decline in five days; while bank stocks in general hit new lows.

Let us here briefly examine the Clearing House figures for

[14] Gibbons, *op. cit.*, p. 364.

the period from August 22 to September 26, as shown in round numbers:

Week Ending:	*Loans*	*Specie*	*Circulation*	*Deposits*
August 22	$120,140,000	$10,097,000	$8,694,000	$64,241,000
August 29	116,589,000	9,241,000	8,671,000	60,861,000
September 5	112,221,000	10,228,000	8,673,000	57,261,000
September 12	109,986,000	12,182,000	8,322,000	57,334,000
September 19	108,777,000	13,556,000	8,074,000	57,852,000
September 26	107,791,000	13,327,000	7,838,000	56,919,000

Perhaps the most significant fact that comes to light in this parallel observation of trends is that while the banks were forcing a merciless contraction of their loans to the extent of more than $12,000,000 in five weeks, the confidence of the public was still persisting at a remarkably high level. Depositors were withdrawing less from the banks each week than the banks were withdrawing from them.

Since deposits and circulation are the basis of a bank's loans and specie, it is evident that the loss of basis during this five-week period was $8,178,000, while the loans were reduced by $12,348,000. Taking into consideration the increase of specie reserved from the liquidations, it becomes apparent that the true relative decrease is $15,578,000. The most violent action was between September 5 and September 19, when the loans were reduced $3,444,000 in the face of an increase of deposits of nearly $600,000. Here again, taking into consideration the increase of specie, the true relative change is represented by a reduction of $6,172,000 in the loans, while the deposits actually increased by $591,000.

In furtherance of the contention that the banks and not the depositors took the lead in forcing liquidation, Gibbons argues that the fall in deposits to the extent of $7,322,000 is by no means wholly traceable to frightened New York merchants. Fully three fourths of this amount, he declares, was drawn out by the country banks, so that the amount withdrawn by the individual dealers was not above $2,000,000.[15]

[15] Gibbons, *op. cit.*, p. 354.

The banknote currency of the city of New York proved during these trying weeks to be the most stable of all forms of credit then in existence. Of an average circulation of $8,000,000, only $1,000,000 was returned for redemption in 1857, in the face of an unparalleled depreciation of every other token of credit even including state bonds and mortgages on real estate. This return, moreover, was made not by individuals through alarm, but mostly by country banks to meet their bills of exchange.[16]

Despite the soundness of New York's own currency, the city itself, as well as the nation at large, found its woes very much increased by the confused and unreliable banknote issues emanating from other parts of the country, particularly the West. Nothing contributed to the crisis more than the wholesale rejection by the redeeming banks of bills which they had been accustomed to receive on deposit. It meant that the bulk of the currency in many sections became practically worthless except at large concessions from their face value. Had it been possible to remove all other causes of excitement, that condition alone would probably have made suspension inevitable.

The suspension in Philadelphia on the twenty-fifth, which resulted largely from the currency problem, had immediate repercussions in New York. It delivered the last telling blow to public confidence which had persisted so miraculously against the rising tide of insolvency. All hope disappeared.

The Street was quick to sense the collapse of spirit, and in a concerted effort to restore confidence the presidents of thirteen New York banks formally declared on September 28 that they would not suspend. Depositors greeted this with deaf ears and began withdrawing currency and specie at an alarming rate. In the week preceding October 3 they inflicted upon the banks the first of a series of three smashing blows by withdrawing more than $4,000,000.

Meanwhile, September 29 witnessed the outbreak of intense

[16] Gibbons, *op. cit.*, p. 394.

panic in Chicago, where business houses were falling at an appalling rate. The same day, in New York, the Erie Railroad, under extreme pressure, called an emergency meeting of stockholders. Money was virtually unobtainable at any price. October 1 saw the suspension of four banks in Louisville, while the stock market skidded to new lows. Erie sold at 10½, a loss of 2½ points in two days; New York Central dropped to 54, a loss of 6 points in two days. Bank stocks fell sharply. The next day was marked by absolute frenzy. Michigan Central fell 10 percent under the cancellation of its October dividend. The Farmers and Mechanics Bank of Williamsburgh suspended. The old and respected business houses of P. Choteau, Jr. and Company and Clark, Dodge and Company, of New York, and Lawrence Stone and Company, of Boston, all went to the wall in the space of two days. Reading was off 5½ points to 31; and New York Central off 3, to 51.

On October 6 the great Pacific Coast house of Willets and Company stopped payment, and the American Exchange Bank refused the drafts of one of the leading banking houses of California. Money was next to impossible at any price in New York. Three Hartford banks suspended.

Storm clouds gathered furiously over New York's financial scene during the next two days. Stock traders became demoralized, and business failures were announced on every side. On the ninth, in the face of runs on the Park Bank and the Bowery Bank, the New York bank officers met in a vain effort to decide upon a course of action. Only confusion resulted. The following day was by far the worst since the revulsion began. Three great railroad companies, the Erie, the Michigan Central, and the Illinois Central, failed to meet their engagements. There was general paralysis everywhere. A score of important houses failed, and runs were started on several of the savings banks.

After a dismal Sabbath, the stock market opened on October 12 in a state of complete anarchy. The Grocers Bank suspended, but the officers of other New York banks met at the

Clearing House in a final Spartan gesture and passed a resolution to continue specie payments to the last. The resolution was short-lived. Next morning the weekly statement for the week ending October 10 revealed still another $4,000,000 contraction and a drop in deposits of about $3,000,000. At ten in the morning a run of depositors for gold began on all the weaker banks in New York, and before the hour of closing twenty of them were compelled to suspend. Thirty continued payment to the close and might have continued longer, but that evening, at a meeting of all the bank officers, it was ascertained that the total amount of gold in the remaining banks was little more than $5,750,000. Consequently a general suspension of specie payment was resolved upon and announced the next morning. All suspended with the single exception of the Chemical, which had also held out in 1837. The Boston banks followed suit, so that by the evening of the fourteenth suspension was general throughout the nation.[17]

The whole monetary system of the United States has fallen with a mighty crash, and now lies before us a magnificent and melancholy ruin [said an article in *Hunt's Merchants' Magazine*]. Yet the country in all its industrial interests was never in a better condition. Our agricultural products are so abundant as absolutely to choke the ordinary channels of transportation. Our manufactures are most successful, and we have the grandest commercial marine on the globe. We are at peace in our own borders, and at peace with all mankind; yet in the twinkling of an eye, we are plunged into the lowest depths of commercial embarrassment, and stand before the world a nation of bankrupts! [18]

It is a gloomy moment in history [commented *Harper's Weekly*]. Not for many years—not in the lifetime of most men who read this paper—has there been so much grave and deep apprehension; never has the future seemed to incalculable as at this time. . . . There is universal commercial prostration and panic, and thou-

[17] *Hunt's Merchants' Magazine*, XXXVII, 583; among the few banks besides the Chemical which weathered the storm were the Indiana State Bank, the Kentucky banks, and four of the New Orleans banks. *Ibid.*

[18] *Ibid.*, XXXVII, 529.

sands of our poorest fellow citizens are turned out against the approaching Winter without employment and without the prospect of it.[19]

Measured by business stagnation and human suffering, the revulsion reached its peak during the two-month period between October 14, when suspension became complete, and December 14, when specie payment was resumed. Trade was literally paralyzed from Bangor to New Orleans.

Our manufacturers [said President Buchanan, reviewing the crisis] everywhere suffered severely, not because of the recent reduction in the tariff duties on imports, but because there was no demand at any price for their production. . . . It is self-evident that where there is no ability to purchase manufactured articles these cannot be sold, and consequently must cease to be produced.[20]

With people obliged to restrict their purchases to articles of prime necessity, all business was at a standstill, but in the general depression the iron manufacturers in the various states probably suffered more than any other class. "There could be no demand for railroad iron," said Buchanan, "after our magnificent system of railroads, extending its benefits to every portion of the Union, had been brought to a dead pause." [21]

Prices of everything declined accordingly. People who expected pork to sell at $24 per barrel found its value reduced to $15. Their flour, instead of selling at $10, had to be sold at $5 to $6; their wheat at $1.25 to $1.35 instead of $2; sugar at 5½ cents to 7 cents, instead of 12 to 13 cents; and other articles in about the same proportion.[22] According to the report of the Secretary of the Treasury, the decline in prices of leading articles from the year ending June 30, 1857, to that ending June 30, 1858, was as follows: wheat flour, 24 percent; hemp, 36 percent; molasses, 34 percent; bar iron, 12 percent; wool, 16 percent; rice, 13½ percent; pork, 9 percent; butter, 10 per-

19 *Harper's Weekly*, Oct. 10, 1857.

20 See *Second Annual Message*, Dec. 6, 1858. Richardson, *Messages and Papers*, V, 520.

21 *Ibid.*

22 New York *Herald*, Aug. 22, 1858.

cent; hay, 20 percent; sugar, 20 percent; pig iron, 15 percent; leather, 17 percent; whale oil, 19 percent; tobacco, 12 percent; copper, 17 percent; cheese, 26 percent.

The following extract from the private correspondence of a wealthy citizen affords an interesting view of the effect of the panic on all classes:

> There was never so much mental suffering in any two months as in the last five weeks. Think of men who never thought of want, except as the proud angels think of suffering—as something fit only for the lower classes—now left without a dollar! The man who refused $30,000 for his house in Temple Place, when he wanted to sell before he went to Europe, saw it knocked down at auction for $19,000. Michigan State bonds have gone down from $1.25 to 66 cents. All property is depreciated. My income will not be half this year what it was last. But, "I still live"; only I shall buy no books; and it makes a gap in my charities.[23]

John Thompson, publisher of the famous *Bank Note Reporter,* authority on values of current and uncurrent bills throughout the country, was utterly ruined by the failure of the Ohio Life. Shortly afterwards he disappeared, and for two months his whereabouts was shrouded in mystery until one day he was discovered in a dingy flat in Greenwich Street, superintending the manufacture of candles from Breckenridge coal oil.[24]

Hundreds of thousands of idle men throughout the nation, who were ready and willing to undertake anything, were faced with the distressing prospect of a winter of desperate privation.[25] In New York City alone the number of unemployed was estimated at close to 100,000,[26] of which nearly 20,000 were thrown out of work within a single fortnight.[27] "Numerous immigrants [from Europe] who have gone to the United States," wrote Evans, "in the flattering expectation of having

[23] O. B. Frothingham, *Life of Theodore Parker,* letter of Oct. 19, 1857, p. 464.

[24] New York *Herald,* Oct. 18, 1857.

[25] *Hunt's Merchants' Magazine,* XLI, 185.

[26] *Ibid.,* p. 189.

[27] *Ibid.,* XXXVII, 532.

full employment in the various arts and trades, have realized disappointed hopes and broken spirits." [28] In the midst of such conditions, considerable radical agitation took place within the ranks of the trade unions. There were meetings and parades, placards with inflammatory inscriptions, and resolutions demanding work and the despoiling of the rich. On one occasion 40,000 unemployed workmen marched through the streets of New York to the City Hall doors, carrying banners reading "Hunger is a sharp thorn" and "We want work." [29] The closest approach to an actual conflict came on November 10, when hungry, overwrought crowds gathered in Wall Street and threatened to make a forced entry into the Sub-Treasury and Custom House to confiscate the $20,000,000 stored in their vaults.[30] Squads of soldiers and marines, however, arrived on the scene in time to protect the government cash reserves.

Nearly every city adopted special relief measures. In Chicago, for instance, where 20,000 men were out of work during the winter, the city council reduced the wages of street cleaners from 75 cents to 50 cents a day and used the funds to spread relief to hungry families.[31]

Considering its lasting effects upon industrial and mercantile interests and upon property owners large and small, the financial crisis itself was of relatively short duration. The Clearing House figures for the closing months of the year are worthy of examination at this juncture:

Week Ending:	*Loans*	*Specie*	*Circulation*	*Deposits*
October 3	$105,935,000	$11,400,000	$7,916,000	$52,798,000
October 10	101,917,000	11,476,000	7,524,000	49,745,000
October 17	97,246,000	7,843,000	8,087,000	42,696,000
October 24	95,593,000	10,411,000	6,884,000	47,873,000
October 31	95,317,000	12,883,000	6,334,000	51,583,000

[28] Evans, *op. cit.*, p. 103.

[29] Sandburg, *Abraham Lincoln—The Prairie Years,* II, 106.

[30] *Bankers' Magazine*, XII, 600; A. C. Cole, *The Irrepressible Conflict, 1850–1865*, pp. 32–34.

[31] Sandburg, *loc. cit.* On this point see J. R. Commons and others, *History of Labor in the United States*, I, 607–10.

Week Ending:	*Loans*	*Specie*	*Circulation*	*Deposits*
November 7	95,866,000	16,492,000	6,434,000	56,424,000
November 14	95,239,000	19,451,000	6,258,000	60,601,000
November 21	95,375,000	23,167,000	6,283,000	64,917,000
November 28	94,963,000	24,303,000	6,520,000	64,307,000
December 5	96,333,000	26,069,000	6,555,000	64,444,000
December 12	96,526,000	26,058,000	6,348,000	62,908,000
December 19	97,211,000	27,957,000	6,309,000	63,710,000
December 26	97,902,000	27,142,000	6,352,000	65,239,000

It will be observed that between the tenth and the seventeenth of October $7,000,000 in deposits were withdrawn, while specie was depleted by more than $2,500,000. A glance at the figures for the following week, however, will excite surprise at the speed with which these losses were recovered. Despite continued depression in the loan column, the specie and deposit columns give evidence of an almost phenomenal restoration of solid resources and public confidence. From these tables it appears that the panic had much the same qualities as an earthquake—a series of preliminary tremors which caused collapse in scattered sections of the commercial structure; then, a single violent shock in which a great deal more of the structure tumbled; then dead calm, a universal sense of relief, and an immediate drive to repair the damage. In one more important aspect the analogy likewise holds. When damage is extensive, its effects are felt and its traces are in evidence long after rehabilitation has begun. So it was with the panic of 1857.

The panic faded almost immediately from the Wall Street consciousness. The same Stock Exchange which had witnessed ruinous depreciations in value during the six weeks prior to the suspension was the scene of an equally remarkable rebound. Twenty-four hours after the suspension, American Exchange bank stock had risen 50 percent.[32] Other issues were correspondingly bullish. The trend continued generally upward during the next several weeks. New York Central, which had fallen 20 points in the two months prior to October 14, had

[32] *Hunt's Merchants' Magazine*, XXXIX, 702–7; Perkins, *Wall Street Panics*, pp. 49–55.

recovered 15 of them by November 20; Reading, which had slumped from 72 to 29, was back to 47¾; Chicago and Rock Island, down from 94¾ to 62, was up again at 82; and Delaware and Hudson, which had tumbled from 118¼ to 75, was back to 101.[33]

Meanwhile the New York banks were not idle. Immediately following their suspension they resolved to receive at par all the secured currency of the banks of the state, so as to enable the country institutions to provide the relief necessary to the restoration of confidence. It was reasoned that the country banks could thus issue their bills, secured by state stocks deposited with the comptroller, to all solvent operators who desired to purchase produce in the West. Thus scattered through the West, these bills would in turn be paid by the producer to the merchant and would be remitted by him to liquidate his debt to the city; they would then be paid into the city banks, would be equalized among these in their settlements at the Clearing House, and would be redeemed by the country banks in drafts on the city against the produce thus purchased and sent forward.[34]

The measure accomplished all which the most sanguine could have expected. The city banks continued the accommodation until the volume of the country money amounted to nearly $8,000,000. On November 18 they ceased to take country currency at par, agreeing to retain all on hand until January, 1858, with interest upon it at 6 percent after December 1, the country banks redeeming at least 20 percent of it per month, beginning January 1.[35]

The plan for a speedy resumption of specie payment by the New York banks was bulwarked during the weeks following the suspension by a continuous flow of gold from California and abroad. It arrived in such quantities by land and sea that

[33] F. L. Eames, *The New York Stock Exchange*, p. 38.

[34] *Hunt's Merchants' Magazine*, XXXVII, 583.

[35] *Ibid.*, p. 711; U.S. Treas. Dept., *Annual Report on Condition of State Banks, 1858*.

the aggregate of $7,843,000 in bank vaults on October 17 had been more than trebled by the end of November. Never in history had the New York banks experienced such a rapid accumulation of gold; and the approach of their bank bills to specie was aided by the fact that exchanges throughout the country were in their favor.[36]

On the fourteenth of December, therefore, exactly two months after total suspension had been declared, the banks of New York resumed specie payment. The effect of this step was immediately felt in other cities. Confidence was so nearly restored by the end of the year that the banks of Boston, those of a large part of New York State and New England, as well as those in New Orleans [37] were likewise paying specie in full. The banks of Providence resumed on January 13, those of Philadelphia and Baltimore on the third and fifth of February, those of Virginia on the first of May, and the remainder before midsummer.[38]

36 *Bankers' Magazine*, XII, 600.

37 The New Orleans banks had all resumed by Nov. 10, a month ahead of the New York banks.

38 *Bankers' Magazine*, XIII, 573.

CHAPTER FIVE

RECOVERY

THE BANKS had scarcely resumed specie payment before numerous explanations for the panic began to be made.[1] *Hunt's Merchants' Magazine* declared it "apparent as the light of day" that the cause of all the confusion was nothing more or less than a "fictitious currency—a currency almost destitute of the element of value, and, of course, a currency on which no safe reliance can ever be placed—a currency which always fails when most needed, which gives the greatest possible facilities for getting into trouble, and least for getting out." [2]

Others argued, on the other hand, that the crisis might have been averted had not the New York banks themselves led the stampede. Their violent efforts to effect an immediate reduction of loans directly after the Ohio Life's failure were declared a grievous mistake. Even taking into account "the previous destruction of value which the credit system had mitigated and concealed," members of the New York press were agreed that "the practical effect of the contraction has been to reduce the quantity of money in circulation by millions of dollars. Hence the scarcity of the article—hence the bankruptcy, the panics, the paralysis." [3]

In a report to subscribers which bitterly attacked the failure of the banks to assist the Ohio Life to meet its obligations and "thus preserve business and credit all over the country," the Mercantile Agency, of New York, wrote in January, 1858:

1 See the excellent article by Samuel Rezneck, "Depression and American Opinion, 1857–1859," *The Journal of Economic History*, II, 1–23.

2 *Hunt's Merchants' Magazine*, XXXVII, 529.

3 Members of the New York Press, *Panics and Revulsions in the United States.*

We entertain the common opinion that the action of the officers of four or five of our strongest banks was the chief cause of the great disasters of the season. They concerted together and forced a rapid and merciless contraction upon all our city banks, carrying along with them those of the whole country.

The report further argued that the larger part of the contraclion could be shown to have been caused by "terror inspired by a trifling cause or misapprehension of danger" in view of the "small losses our banks have met with, and the quickness with which they were able to collect in and place themselves in a strong position." [4]

Amasa Walker, the economist, was more lenient:

Let us not find fault with those who have been called to act as officers of banking institutions in the present crisis. No class of men have been placed in more embarrassing circumstances. We have no occasion for censure. It was natural that they should struggle long, however hopelessly, to save the credit of their banks. They have done so. It was their fortune to be connected with the most vicious system of banking economy that the world ever saw, and they have conducted probably as well as any other men would in their positions.[5]

The New York *Herald* sympathized with the Walker point of view. The banks, it held, were guilty of nothing more than hastening the upheaval. The die had long since been cast. "The reaction," said the *Herald,* "was as necessary as a thunder-storm in a mephitic and unhealthy atmosphere. It purified the commercial and financial elements, and tended to restore vitality and health, alike conducive to regular trade, found progress, and permanent prosperity." [6]

J. S. Gibbons, in reviewing the economic picture from the time of the establishment of the Clearing House Association in 1854, makes an extremely significant observation. He points

[4] *Hunt's Merchants' Magazine,* XXXVII, 534. [5] *Ibid.*

[6] Aug. 22, 1858; see W. B. Smith and A. H. Cole, *Fluctuations in American Business, 1790–1860,* pp. 131–32, for an examination of the charges that the banks were responsible for the panic.

out with the aid of graphs that at the beginning a harmonious relationship existed among deposits, loans, and specie. All three rose and fell together throughout the fluctuations of the financial market. During the year ending with July, 1855, the specie was kept at 25 percent of the deposits. The Association's balance wheel was perfect insofar as it prevented individual members going astray, but the graph for subsequent years reveals that for want of a fixed scale it did not prevent the whole from going astray together. In August, 1855, the specie line fell below the scale and did not again ascend to it until after the suspension in October, 1857. The average of specie with respect to the deposits sank from 25 percent in 1854–55 to 21 percent in 1855–56 and to 18 percent in 1856–57, while the loans were steadily on the increase. Had the ratio of coin to the whole resources for the year 1854–55 been preserved in the following years, there would have been but $85,000,000 of loans on the actual specie of 1855–56, whereas there were $100,000,000; and it would have admitted but $76,000,000 of loans on the actual coin of 1856–57, whereas there were $111,000,000. In other words, the loans of 1855–56 were $15,000,000 in excess of the scale, and the loans of 1856-57 were $35,000,000 in excess.[7]

This was the extent to which credit had been overexpanded during the years of extravagance and speculation which preceded the crisis. A mountain of debt had been carried along in the volume of trade. Extravagances had sapped the foundations of commercial success in hundreds of instances in which credit supplied the place of lost capital. And when the crisis came it brought to light the countless indiscretions of the merchant whose capital had been sunk or withdrawn from legitimate use for investment in some dazzling speculation. It revealed that his bills payable represented not only his mer-

[7] James Sloan Gibbons, *The Banks of New York and the Panic of 1857*, p 365. For a check on Gibbons consult A. H. Cole, "The New York Money Market, 1843–1862," in *Review of Economic Statistics*, XI, 167; Dunbar, *Economic Essays*, p. 287.

chandise debt but his debt for sunken capital, railroad stocks, worthless real estate, and extravagant living. It would not be unreasonable to estimate that the $122,000,000 of bills payable, constituting the New York bank loans of August, 1857, were scarcely more than one fourth of the personal debt then current among the city's population. The rest floated in other channels, in the hands of private capitalists, in trust and insurance companies, in open-book accounts, and in foreign banks.[8] The same conditions held true throughout the nation, with a few notable exceptions.

Small wonder, then, that the effects of the panic did not cease with the renewal of confidence in the Stock Exchange or even with the complete resumption of specie payment. The panic was soon over, but the depression lingered on. As already noted, the crash had brought about an enormous curtailment of production, decimation of profits, discharge of workers, and consequent destruction of purchasing power. Protracted stagnation of business was inevitable.[9]

Though the panic was over with the resumption of specie payment if not sooner, the depression lasted through 1858 and in some localities well into 1859. For obvious reasons some sections of the nation suffered more acutely and for a longer period than others. Under the blight of a collapsed real-estate bubble, poor crops, decline in grain prices, a degenerate currency, and a heterogeneous banking structure, the Middle West was by far the hardest hit. Contrary to long prevailing opinion, the South, especially southern centers such as Charleston and New Orleans, suffered rather severely. The eastern states, despite the severity of the blow, exhibited remarkable recuperative powers. Only California escaped practically unscathed.

An idea of the severity of the crisis in the West is given by

[8] Gibbons, *op. cit.*, p. 374; C. F. Dunbar, *Economic Essays*, pp. 279–82.

[9] Even as late as Jan. 1, 1859, the New York *Tribune* reported that the prospect was not hopeful: "Immigration has almost ceased. Wages, rents, and profits have greatly fallen."

the Nebraska correspondent of the New York *Herald,* writing in January, 1858:

The hard times in these "diggins" seem "getting no better very fast." Nine-tenths of our people owe, and have no immediate way to pay. Everything in the shape of property is quite low. The merchants here, what few have stood the storm thus far, sell for cash, and the truth is there is very little in the country. Provisions of all kinds still hold up comparatively high. Gambling to a considerable extent is carried on here, as usual. The shinplaster bills entitled "Omaha City Scrip" are worth but about 48 cents on the dollar.[10]

A whole year after the resumption of the specie payment the people of the West were still dolefully contemplating the ravages of the panic, according to the New York *Tribune* for Christmas Day, 1858: "Railroads partly constructed and there stopped for want of means; blocks of buildings ditto; counties and cities involved by the issue of railroad bonds and practically insolvent; individuals striving to stave off the satisfaction of debts, obligations, judgments, executions—such is the all but universal condition."

The fact that the western farmer was a heavy plunger in railroad securities during the boom made his plight worse. To quote from one of Wisconsin's county newspapers:

In the town of Polk [Wisconsin] a farmer mortgaged his farm for stock in the La Crosse Railroad to the amount of $2,000. The *Democrat* calculates with the interest on the mortgages, the future probable valuation of his farm, and the present rates of the stock, the farmer will lose $2,340 by the operation. Our agricultural friend is somewhat in the situation of a man who had an enraged tiger by the tail—extremely dangerous to hold on, and certain death to let go.

It is said that from 2,000 to 3,000 farms are thus mortgaged to railroads in Wisconsin; that the railroads cannot pay, and to release their farms will strip nine-tenths of them of the hard earnings of many years.[11]

10 Jan. 4, 1858. For decline in grain prices consult W. T. Hutchinson, *Cyrus H. McCormick,* II, 75.

11 Washington County *Democrat,* Dec. 20, 1857.

Many were the growing municipalities which found it necessary to reduce the cost of local government in order to survive. Said the Cincinnati *Gazette,* in discussing the "wise" action of the people of Winona, Minn., in abandoning their city charter and returning to village life: "Poverty reduces big towns as well as big people. As men in 'pinching times' cannot afford to keep the grandest equipage, so small municipalities find it difficult to keep a Mayor and Alderman, a Town Crier and a Scavenger." [12]

Not all sections of the West reacted alike. The larger cities varied widely in their capacity for recuperation. A traveling correspondent of the New York *Times,* writing in the early summer of 1858, draws an interesting contrast between Chicago and Cincinnati:

> Chicago is evidently suffering greatly from the troubles of last year. The rush of several years back has been succeeded by a severe reaction. The hand of improvement is stayed. Rents have fallen. The values of real estate are greatly reduced. Numbers of stores are vacant, and whereas on my former trip in 1856, the whole city seemed as bustling as Broadway, its appearance last week was proportionately like a retired country village.
>
> Cincinnati has resisted the pressure better than any city I know, East or West. A few failures have, it is true, resulted from the commercial tornado which swept over the country last year; but the tokens of general prosperity are too palpable to be overlooked. Although the usual dull season for commercial sales has fairly commenced, there is an evident air of business encircling the city. The iron founders who contribute so largely to the trade of Cincinnati, are in full blast. The furniture makers, another important industrial class, are busily occupied in manufacturing and shipping. Few stores, desirably located, are empty; and dwelling houses are rarely to be found at any price. And so, on every hand, the proofs multiply of the existence, within itself, of elements of wealth and stability and permanent prosperity.[13]

While other sections of the nation were recovering, crop failure and severe drought through wide areas imposed

[12] Dec. 29, 1857. [13] Letter quoted in Cincinnati *Daily Gazette,* July 9, 1858.

further hardships on Mid-Westerners. An Indiana journalist, writing in the spring of 1859, says:

In passing recently through the central portion of the State, we heard men everywhere complaining of the hardness of the times. Every department of business is suffering more or less from the pressure occasioned by the scarcity of grain and provisions in the country. In Clay county, in particular, and other parts, many people are actually suffering. Stock of all kinds—horses, cattle, sheep and hogs—is lying dead in the fence corners of almost every farm, and is constantly dying from starvation. We heard of some men who were glad to furnish cord wood on their own lands, cut and pile it, and sell it on the ground for forty cents a cord, and take pay in grain and provisions, in order to live until another season.[14]

Not all Easterners believed these stories of distress which emanated from the West. "That paradise of usurers," charged Greeley's *Tribune,* was ready "for any preposterous scheme of assumption." "Too many," the *Tribune* went on to say, instead of meeting their creditors "have tried to stave off, and fight executions and invoke the aid of stay laws, and put their property into the hands of relatives or confederates, . . . to the advantage of sheriffs and sharking lawyers, and the disadvantage of every body else." [15]

In contrast with the prolonged depression of the Middle West, conditions in California, source of the nation's gold supply, were virtually unchanged by the crisis. The New York *Herald* observed in January, 1858:

While the panic has swept relentlessly over most of our other states, California seems to have been almost entirely exempted from its effects. Its general condition has never been more substantially prosperous and flourishing than at the present moment. . . . It presents commercially, socially and politically all the evidences of a steady progress. . . . An unmistakable evidence of the growing internal prosperity of the state is to be found in the statement that, while the produce of gold is increasing at a ratio, the amount retained for domestic uses is relatively much larger than it has

[14] Evansville (Indiana) *Inquirer,* April 6, 1859.
[15] New York *Tribune,* Oct. 14, 1857, Dec. 25, 1858.

ever been before. This proves, of course, an augmented activity in all the branches of industrial and commercial operations, as well as a healthy condition of things generally.[16]

With better than average cotton crops during 1856, 1857, and 1858, the South's great staple industry continued to flourish with but a slight fall in prices over a brief period. Nevertheless the South, as we have already observed, did not escape entirely the blighting effects of the panic. Governor McRae of Mississippi, addressing the legislature a few weeks after the failure of the Ohio Life, gave thanks that his state had rid itself some fifteen years earlier of the evils of a paper currency, but noted with alarm that the country's monetary system had a pernicious effect on all sections. Cotton, he said, would not then command more than two thirds of its actual intrinsic market value, owing to the general failure of the banking system and the consequent destruction of confidence throughout the whole country.[17]

The revival, however, was rapid and foreign trade brisk, so that cotton, together with the South's other basic staples—sugar, tobacco, rice, and hemp—remained almost the only articles of commerce to escape the effects of the world-wide slump.

Where the influence of northern banking was too intimate to permit of escape, bank failures and suspensions did occur, it is true. But on November 10 the New Orleans *Picayune* declared with pride:

The few banks in our city that suspended specie payment in October, viz.: Bank of New Orleans, Union Bank, Mechanics' and Traders' Bank, and Citizens' Bank, have all resumed specie payments. The resumption in full of the Citizens' Bank has been accompanied by an increase in her coin of more than a million dollars, and followed by an increase of deposits to nearly seven

[16] Jan. 18, 1858.

[17] *Annual Message to the Mississippi Legislature,* Nov. 3, 1857. See Dunbar, *op. cit.,* pp. 291 ff., for opinion that the South was less affected by the depression than the rest of the country.

hundred thousand dollars, with a curtailment of her loans of about $370,000.

In the process of healthy reaction, the banks are stronger than they were when the northern suspensions alarmed the sensitive billholder, and caused that senseless run which produced so much mischief. The steadiness with which these banks sustained themselves against the shock, and the strength with which they have righted themselves so speedily, are proofs of the intrinsic excellence of the principles upon which they are organized; and the endurance and success with which the commercial community stood up under the intense pressure which these curtailments called for, are titles to confidence of inestimable value to their future prosperity and that of the city.

An aristocratic confidence in its own superiority over the get-rich-quick inhabitants of the North was the general feeling in the conservative, slaveholding South. Its greater prosperity seemed solid enough foundation for the exultant cry of Hammond of South Carolina in the Senate:

Cotton is king! Who can doubt it that has looked upon recent events? When the abuse of credit annihilated confidence . . . when you came to a deadlock and revolutions were threatened, what brought you up? Fortunately for you it was the commencement of the cotton season and we have poured upon you one million six hundred thousand bales of cotton just at the crisis to save you.[18]

"The wealth of the South," said *DeBow's Review* for December, 1857, "is permanent and real, that of the North fugitive and fictitious. Events now transpiring are exposing the fiction as humbug after humbug explodes." [19]

The superior prosperity of the southern states is further indicated by the fact that construction there was not affected by the panic, but went on at a more rapid rate than before.

[18] *Congressional Globe*, 35th Cong., 1st Sess., p. 961.

[19] Vol. XXIII, p. 592. The favorable position of the South following the panic induced many northern spokesmen, including the New York *Herald*, to plead for a cessation of sectional animosity. "Nigger Agitation" should cease and "Bleeding Kansas" should be forgotten. See New York *Herald*, Sept. 29, Oct. 7, 22, 25, 1857.

The southern railway connections between the Atlantic seaboard and the interior were completed, the system of roads from Virginia and South Carolina reaching Memphis on the Mississippi through Chattanooga in 1858 and 1859. Still the South remained far behind the North as a whole, having less than a third of the total railway mileage.[20]

In view of such variable geographic and industrial factors, it is difficult to estimate the duration of the so-called period of depression which followed the panic. In certain areas recovery was complete early in 1858; elsewhere the depression extended late into 1859. But, whatever its duration, such a period was necessary to restore trade and commerce to their healthy and legitimate channels. As the *Herald* put it, "it was necessary to bring about a greater equality between the value of labor and the value of products to be given in exchange for it, and free them from the disturbing influence of the unnatural expansion of credit." [21]

By early January the foreign exchanges were showing marked improvement, and by the last of the month Sterling bills had reached as high as 110, an above-normal rate. In New York the interest due on state bonds was punctually met, with the result that their value recovered nearly 15 percent from the October prices.[22] An editorial in the *Herald,* January 6, offered this sanguine comment:

> Strong symptoms of revival in every line are daily manifesting themselves. The bullion in the vaults of the banks is steadily increasing and now reaches an aggregate of $30,000,000. Trade and commerce bid fair to start earlier than usual, and one of the strongest evidences of their revival is the expansion of crinoline.

A month later the same paper commented at greater length on what it termed the "palpable signs of a wholesome recovery." Since the revulsion had tended to force specie to the financial centers, the Clearing House was experiencing a decided increase in volume of business. Of the $83,000,000 held

20 *8th Census,* Miscellaneous Statistics, p. 323.

21 Aug. 22, 1858.

22 *Bankers' Magazine,* XIII, 574.

by the banks of the nation, New York had $30,000,000 and in consequence was increasing its discounts and affording every facility to young houses to embark in trade. "All this money could not lie idle," said the *Herald:*

We have seen, and are still seeing its effect upon the stock market, in reviving confidence, and inflating every dividend-paying security; though this may, and naturally will, continue throughout the spring and summer, the stock market cannot alone afford employment for such amounts of capital as are now lying idle in the banks. Trade alone can make it pay interest, and trade is accordingly on the mend.[23]

Among the improvements recorded in February was the establishment in Philadelphia of a clearing house system founded upon the one which had been in existence in New York since 1853. Another was the resumption of payment on the twentieth by the Michigan Central Railroad of its past due obligations. Improvement in the stock market likewise continued, until by the end of April the price of New York Central shares was up to 89 from a low of 52, Erie to 25 from a low of 10, and other issues correspondingly strong. There was a slight but not serious decline in some of the railroad securities in May.

The newspapers and financial publications of July and August make frequent reference to the reduction in unemployment—a healthy sign which was general in most important branches of industry.[24] Simultaneously eastern dealers were looking optimistically upon the increased flow of business in grains, corn, flour, lumber, pork, beef, and hides, and, to a lesser degree, iron.[25]

The swing toward recovery, particularly in the East, was so pronounced during the rest of the year that President Buchanan, in his second annual message to Congress, made the following comment:

[23] New York *Herald*, Feb. 7, 1858.

[24] *Bankers' Magazine*, XIII, 579; New York *Times*, July 12, 1858; Philadelphia *Ledger*, Aug. 3, 1858.

[25] Cincinnati *Daily Gazette*, Sept. 3, 1858.

The effects of the revulsion are now slowly but surely passing away. The energy and enterprise of our citizens, with our unbounded resources, will within the period of another year restore a state of wholesome industry and trade.[26]

An interesting index of the trend is found in the following comparative table of failures of banks and mercantile firms during the years 1857 and 1858. The totals for the entire nation show only a slight reduction in the number of failures, but the aggregate losses in dollars were reduced by more than 64 percent.[27]

State	*1857*	*Total Liabilities*	*1858*	*Total Liabilities*
New York	1,586	$150,619,000	866	$24,352,020
Pennsylvania	534	36,420,000	363	14,260,783
Ohio	346	6,868,000	282	3,273,371
Indiana	139	1,636,000	127	1,154,684
Illinois	316	9,348,000	392	8,568,874
Michigan	132	2,518,000	147	2,779,404
Iowa	144	2,068,000	120	3,021,180
Wisconsin	120	1,624,000	158	2,750,298
Minnesota and Territories	63	1,705,000	90	1,365,840
Delaware and District of Columbia	20	261,000	46	277,150
Massachusetts	483	43,621,000	251	6,116,717
Rhode Island	39	4,669,000	30	647,923
Connecticut	61	1,129,000	89	2,213,430
Maine	81	1,000,000	61	646,051
New Hampshire	70	928,000	37	403,152
Vermont	57	473,000	40	278,720
New Jersey	86	1,142,000	60	775,800
Louisiana	63	6,531,000	58	3,806,900
Missouri	69	5,955,000	51	1,398,980
Maryland	99	3,931,000	168	2,963,606
Kentucky	50	1,764,000	80	1,237,462
Virginia	120	1,763,000	269	2,682,925
Georgia	32	925,000	71	1,415,243
Arkansas	7	309,000	17	739,500
Alabama	16	295,000	48	2,038,752
Mississippi	11	445,000	36	1,053,000
Tennessee	40	712,000	103	1,597,015
Texas	15	293,000	28	467,432
North Carolina	62	1,171,000	90	1,499,400
South Carolina	55	1,227,000	41	828,080
Florida	7	250,000	6	142,440
Total in the United States	4,932	$291,750,000	4,225	$95,749,662

This table bears out what has already been said regarding the severity of the depression in the West as compared with

[26] Dec. 6, 1858. See Richardson, *op. cit.*, V, 521.

[27] Table printed in *Bankers' Magazine*, XIII, 641–43.

other sections of the country. While the thickly populated states of New York, Massachusetts, and Pennsylvania were recording a marked improvement, such areas as Michigan, Iowa, Wisconsin, and Minnesota were still in great straits. Conditions in Michigan were aggravated by a poor wheat crop and a depressed lumber business; Iowa, with equally bad crops, had no banks of issue and found itself virtually without a circulating medium, since capital had a tendency to flow away to the financial centers in other parts of the nation. Wisconsin, where so many depended upon the lumber trade for a living, saw a 23-percent increase in failure during 1858. Minnesota, where trade had prospered from the continuous flow of immigration, found itself relatively deserted and its population financially shackled by the collapse of the real-estate bubble.

The year 1858 saw an advance of from 8 to 12 percent in most railway stocks. Of equal significance are the following changes in the public stock of the several states, from the quotations listed for December 31, 1857, and December 31, 1858: [28]

	1857	*1858*
Virginia	99	99½
Missouri	80½	90½
Tennessee	83	95
New York 6's	108	115
California	65½	92
Ohio	100	108
North Carolina	90	100½
Georgia	92	102

And the following prices of regular dividend shares and mortgages for the same dates: [29]

	1857	*1858*
Panama	94½	123½
Pacific Mail	67	91
Illinois Central 7's	84	87½
Michigan Central 8's	84	96
New York Central 6's	81	90½
New York Central	74	84⅔
Harlem firsts	67	89½
Hudson firsts	96	104½
Brooklyn 6's	90	103

28 New York *Daily Times*, Jan. 3, 1859.

29 *Ibid.*

"The financial crisis of 1857, which threatened to paralyze the whole enterprise of this country, and to disturb the trade of the world for a long time to come, has become almost a matter of history," said the New York *Daily Times* on New Year's Day, 1859. In a tone of brightest optimism, the article told how the spindles were flying again in New England and how the ironmasters of Pennsylvania were reporting themselves equal to supplying the whole continent with railways of the finest quality and at the fairest price. With the renewed demand for our staples of export, there was fresh activity in all the industrial centers and additional stimulus to agriculture and inland trade. "Capital which was frightened back a year ago upon its citadels," said the *Times,* "begins to venture out once more."

From the South came this buoyant report of conditions in March, 1859:

There is no disputing the fact that the southern portion of the Confederacy is in a highly prosperous condition—perhaps never more so. Of all the great staples produced, the crops during the past year have been abundant, sales active, and prices high. No species of property has felt the effect of this state of affairs more sensibly than the negroes. The average price of field hands may be stated at $1500 and the tendency is upward. A-1 niggers sell for $1750 to $2000. These rates were never reached but once before, and that was during the speculative times of 1836. The South is getting out of debt and beginning to accumulate surplus capital.[30]

The spring of 1859 witnessed a revival of activity in certain sections of the West as well. On March 20 the St. Louis *Republican* wrote jubilantly:

On Main Street we never saw better signs of a large healthy trade, and on inquiry we learned that the outward signs did not deceive us. From one end of the street to the other, so far as wholesale houses extended, there were piles upon piles of boxes of dry goods, saddlery, hardware, drugs and paints, hats and hatters' trimmings, and generally every description of goods with which the stores on that street are so well filled. They were marked for Fort Smith and

[30] New York *Daily Times,* New Orleans correspondent, March 25, 1859.

other towns in Arkansas, for Kansas and Nebraska territories, for Iowa and Illinois, and large amounts for Missouri. The sales of this week, in the dry goods line, will, it is very probable, be heavier than those of any week of the present season.

In April, 1859, we read that New Yorkers were "catching their breaths with enthusiasm at the flush times ahead. In the language of the favorite organ of this prosperity," wrote a Philadelphia journal, "they are 'close upon a repetition of the flush times that immediately preceded the crash of 1857.' "[31]

The same journal writes at length upon the vast improvement in commerce in Philadelphia:

> While the sales incident to the spring trade in this city have been unusually large, the external commerce is still more so. During the month of March, this year, there were 1546 arrivals at this port, against 713 for the corresponding month of last year. The improvement is more manifest in the coasting trade, as will be seen by the following: Arrivals coastwise at Philadelphia, for March of this year, 1499; ditto for March of last year, 668; increase 831; equal to much more than a doubling of the coasting trade. In the bulk, too, of the tonnage, as well as in the number of the coastwise, the increase is great. . . . There has been an increase of one ship, five barques, four brigs, 160 schooners, 55 steamers, exclusive of the sloops, barges and boats. . . .
>
> As the above statistics would show, the shipping business of Philadelphia is now quite brisk. Our marine advertisements occupy more space than for a long period heretofore.[32]

Among the many encouraging signs of improved commercial conditions in 1859 was the manufacture of cotton goods in New England. The total consumption of cotton for the first eight months of the year was over 900,000 bales, or about 50 percent more than that of 1858. Even the hard-suffering West began to place large orders, and foreign commerce was brisk. The value of the export of domestic cotton to foreign markets rose from $5,651,504 in 1858 to $8,316,222 in 1859.[33]

[31] Philadelphia *North American and United States Gazette*, April 2, 1859.
[32] *Ibid.* [33] *Bankers' Magazine*, XV, 212.

The year 1859 found the nation returning to normal conlitions. During 1858, for the first time in years, there had been in international balance in favor of the United States, owing o the fact that the decline in imports had been sharper than he decline in exports. Poor harvests in Europe during 1857 vere a contributing factor. In 1859 the flow of imports once nore exceeded exports, thus reëstablishing the United States o the outside world as a gold-producing nation.

At the close of the year 1859 President Buchanan informed Congress that the "general health of the country has been excellent, our harvests have been unusually plentiful, and prosperity smiles throughout the land." [34] And one full year ater, using almost the same words in his fourth annual nessage, he remarked on how that trend had continued durng 1860:

> Throughout the year since our last meeting the country has been eminently prosperous in all its material interests. The general iealth has been excellent, our harvests have been abundant, and plenty smiles throughout the land. Our commerce and manufacures have been prosecuted with energy and industry, and have rielded fair and ample returns. In short, no nation in the tide of ime has ever presented a spectacle of greater material prosperity han we have done.[35]

To what extent the federal government contributed to recovery is difficult to say. Unquestionably certain short-term actors of a political nature, notably the tariff of 1857, Bleedng Kansas, the Dred Scott Decision, and the impending crisis vere factors partly responsible for the panic. That these same tems may have retarded recovery is possible. The messages of President Buchanan and Secretary of the Treasury Howell Cobb abound in comments on their limited powers to deal vith the situation.

Some critics maintain that Cobb as Secretary of the Treasıry proved himself considerably less astute as a financier than

[34] Dec. 19, 1859. See Richardson, *op. cit.*, V, 552.
[35] Dec. 3, 1860. See Richardson, *op. cit.*, V, 626.

as a politician. However true this may be, it is not our intention to pass judgment on his actions. It may be equally true that the effectiveness of both Buchanan and Cobb during the crisis and the subsequent depression was considerably curtailed by the fact that the majority sentiment in both Houses of Congress was northern and consequently not favorable toward the President or his cabinet.

Before Congress met for its winter session in 1857, Cobb made two moves designed to afford relief to public distress. His first was to announce that beginning September 30 the Treasury would start redemption of its 1848 bond issue, due in 1868, so that savings banks would be more easily able to provide gold for their depositors. *Hunt's Merchants' Magazine* said of this: "He did what he legally could for the public relief, and his action saved an immense amount of suffering." [36] And Cobb said of it himself: "The opportunity which it [the Independent Treasury] afforded at an early period of relieving the financial embarrassments of the country by the policy of redeeming a portion of the public debt and furnishing the country thereby with the specie used in its redemption was attended with the happiest results. It is difficult to estimate the extent of the relief which was thus afforded." [37] Of the $10,344,241.80 which was thus redeemed by June 30, 1859, however, only $1,435,900 was redeemed by June 30, 1858.[38]

Cobb's second move toward providing relief was to transfer gold bullion from the United States Assay Office in New York to the mint in Philadelphia for the purpose of increasing the circulation of gold dollars and quarter eagles. A total of approximately $4,000,000 were minted in November in Philadelphia, San Francisco, and New Orleans.[39]

President Buchanan, in his first annual message, December

[36] *Hunt's Merchants' Magazine,* XXXVII, 552.

[37] *Report of the Secretary of the Treasury,* Dec. 6, 1858; *Finance Reports,* 1858–59.

[38] *Ibid.*

[39] The output was as follows: Philadelphia $2,108,426; San Francisco $1,570,000; New Orleans $270,000. *Hunt's Merchants' Magazine,* XXXVII, 72–75.

8, 1857, told Congress that it was the duty of the government by all proper means within its power to aid in alleviating the sufferings of the people occasioned by the suspension of the banks and to provide against a recurrence of the same calamity. "Unfortunately," he continued, "in either aspect of the case, it can do but little." He rested considerable hope on the fact that the disbursements of the Independent Treasury in coin would materially assist in restoring a sound currency.

Having remarked but a few months earlier, upon the occasion of his inaugural, that the nation was "embarrassed from too large a surplus in the Treasury," Buchanan now found the government's coffers draining rapidly. The revenue, chiefly derived from duties on imports, had been greatly reduced because imports themselves had fallen off sharply. Meanwhile the appropriations made by Congress at its previous session had been very large.

> Under these circumstances [said Buchanan], a loan may be required before the close of your present session; but this, although deeply to be regretted, would prove to be only a slight misfortune when compared with the suffering and distress prevailing among the people. With this the government cannot fail deeply to sympathize though it may be without the power to extend relief.[40]

Cobb, in his annual report on the finances issued the following day, echoed Buchanan's opinion that the federal government was strictly limited in what it could do toward the public relief:

> A revulsion in the monetary affairs of the country always occasions more or less of distress among the people. The consequence is that the public mind is directed to the government for relief. . . . They do not stop to inquire into the power which has been conferred by the people upon their agents or the objects for which that power is to be exercised. Their inquiry is limited to the simple fact of existing embarrassments, and they see no other agency capable of affording relief, and their necessities, not their judgments, force them to the conclusion that the government not only

[40] First Annual Message, Dec. 8, 1857. See Richardson, *op. cit.*, V, 437.

can but ought to relieve them. . . . Such is not the true theory of our government. It is one of limited powers. . . . The use of large amounts of money, to be raised either by a loan or the issue of treasury notes, would afford temporary relief to an extent limited only by the discretion of the government in this unauthorized use of the public treasure and credit. But where shall we look for the power to do this in the Constitution?

Congress, attempting to supply the deficiency in the Treasury, authorized, by the Act of December 23, 1857, the issue of $20,000,000 of Treasury notes. Under its terms $6,000,000 of the notes were issued immediately and the remainder as required, after a 30-day period of advertisement. All were to bear a maximum interest of 6 percent and were redeemable after the expiration of one year. The notes were acceptable in payment of debts due the government, and credit was given for the amount of interest due on the note on the day received. Provision was made for the reissuance of other Treasury notes to supplant those which were thus redeemed. The only restriction was that the sum in circulation should at no time exceed $20,000,000. Before the power to issue and reissue expired on January 1, 1859, the Treasury Department had put into circulation a total of $23,716,300 of the notes. Two months later, under a new act of Congress, the power of issue and reissue granted under the previous act was revived and continued in force until July 1, 1860.[41]

Meanwhile, finding that the note issue was inadequate to the needs of the government, Congress authorized, by the Act of June 14, 1858, a loan of $20,000,000 to be applied to the payment of appropriations made by law. Redeemable after fifteen years, the bonds had a minimum denomination of $1,000 and bore 5 percent interest. By the end of the year (December 6, 1858) the President had negotiated $10,000,000 of the loan, and a year later Cobb reported that nearly $19,000,000 in bonds had thus far been subscribed, with the remainder soon

[41] *Report of the Secretary of the Treasury*, March 3, 1859; *Finance Reports*, 1858–59.

to be completed. "This," he pointed out, "will make the permanent public debt 45 million." [42]

Congress had paid little heed to Buchanan's plea in his first annual message for a curtailment of expenditures and even less to the following statement from his message of a year later, which nowadays must seem almost naïve:

> No statesman would advise that we should go on increasing the national debt to meet the ordinary expenses of the government. This would be a most ruinous policy.[43]

Government expenditures, therefore, continued unabated, with the result that repeated issues of bonds and Treasury notes were necessary. On June 22, 1860, another act was passed which authorized the President to borrow up to $21,-000,000 within a year by issuing ten-to-twenty-year bonds in the redemption of outstanding Treasury notes. Government credit, however, remained unimpaired. It was not until after 1860, when civil war threatened, that confidence in government solvency was shaken.

The efforts on the part of the administration toward what Buchanan had termed "providing against a recurrence of the same calamity" were singularly unproductive. Blaming the railroad companies for contributing so largely to "that expansion of credit which is properly chargeable with the recent revulsion," Cobb, in his report of December 8, 1857, contended that the government could do little toward "extricating individuals, corporations, or communities from the pernicious consequences." Urging that a speedy adjustment of the relations between creditor and debtor by liquidation and settlement was necessary to the restoration of the equilibrium, Cobb recommended that Congress enact a compulsory bankrupt law "for the protection of creditors, not the relief of debtors; to prevent improper credit, not to pay improvident debts; compulsory not voluntary." It would serve as an im-

[42] *Ibid.*, Dec. 22, 1859.
[43] Dec. 6, 1858. See Richardson, *op. cit.*, V, 521.

portant check on the banks and railroad corporations, he argued, because of "the immense capital employed by these companies, their controlling power and influence, and their disposition to expand and enlarge their credit."

Congress, however, failed to act even when Buchanan a year later renewed the recommendation for a bankrupt law and qualified his request with the remark: "This is all the direct power over the subject which I believe the Federal Government possesses." [44] The *Herald*, remarking in March that the failures of commercial houses were still going on, had urged:

> There is but one remedy for this, and that is a good bankrupt law, applicable to individuals, banks, railroads, and all corporations. If the houses that are breaking now could have settled with their creditors long ago, by the operation of a bankrupt law, and started afresh, basing their business on the new state of affairs which panics always leave behind them, many of them would be now in a safer and more thriving condition; but by the present system commercial disasters are protracted, but not avoided.[45]

But government control over bankruptcy, which had been repealed in 1843, was not renewed until a Federal Bankrupt Law was enacted March 2, 1867.[46] Insolvent laws, however, prevailed throughout the Union, the various states instituting their own bankrupt systems. In Maine, New Hampshire, Massachusetts, Virginia, and Kentucky the laws were confined to the relief of debtors charged in execution. In New Jersey, Delaware, Maryland, Tennessee, North and South Carolina, Georgia, Alabama, Mississippi, and Illinois the insolvent laws extended to debtors in prison on mesne or final process. In New York, Connecticut, Rhode Island, Pennsylvania, Ohio, Indiana, Missouri, and Louisiana they were still more extensive and reached the debtor whether in or out of prison.[47]

Cobb, enamored of the way the collection and disbursement

[44] *Ibid.* [45] March 12, 1858.

[46] *Federal Statutes*, published by Library of Congress, June, 1926.

[47] *Bankers' Magazine*, XII, 195.

of the public revenue had proceeded without loss or embarrassment, pointed out that the Independent Treasury system had saved the government from resorting to the distressing expedients that had been necessary in 1837. Upon this fact he based a recommendation that the respective state governments should adopt a similar principle and establish independent state treasuries, as a means of securing a sound paper currency.[48] Ohio actually did so in 1858.

Buchanan, as we have said, was so obsessed with the doctrine of states' rights that he insisted upon predicating all his acts and recommendations on the assumption that the federal government was powerless to provide anything of consequence either in the direction of relief or of reform. "No government, and especially a government of such limited powers as that of the United States," said he in his second annual message, "could have prevented the late revulsion. The whole commercial world seemed for years to have been rushing to this catastrophe." [49]

Placing the blame for the revulsion directly upon the extravagant and vicious system of paper currency and bank credits, Buchanan, as we have earlier quoted him, predicted that "these revulsions must continue to recur at successive intervals so long as the amount of the paper currency and bank loans and discounts of the country shall be left to the discretion of 1400 irresponsible banking institutions, which from the very law of their nature will consult the interest of their stockholders rather than the public welfare." [50]

In the same message, however, Buchanan hastened to stress the opinion that "the Federal Government can not do much to provide against a recurrence of existing evils. . . . We must mainly rely upon the patriotism and wisdom of the States for the prevention and redress of the evils." Yet later in the

[48] *Report of the Secretary of Treas.*, Dec. 8, 1857.
[49] Dec. 6, 1858. See Richardson, *op. cit.*, V, 520.
[50] Dec. 8, 1857. See Richardson, *op. cit.*, V, 437.

same message Buchanan went so far as to remark "after long study and much reflection," that: "If experience shall prove it to be impossible to enjoy the facilities which well-regulated banks might afford without at the same time suffering the calamities which the excesses of the banks have hitherto inflicted upon the country, it would be far the lesser evil to deprive them altogether of the power to issue a paper currency and confine them to functions of banks of deposit and discount."

Beyond this point Buchanan's interest and efforts in behalf of banking reform ceased. If his thoughts ever did explore the possibilities of a consolidation of banking interests, it is apparent that they always bogged down into a recollection of the Bank of the United States. At any rate these were his conclusions:

> Even if insurmountable constitutional objections did not exist against the creation of a National Bank, this would furnish no adequate preventive security. The history of the last Bank of the United States abundantly proves the truth of this assertion. Such a bank could not, if it would, regulate the issues and credits of fourteen hundred state banks in such a manner as to prevent the ruinous expansions and contractions in our currency which afflicted the country throughout the existence of the late bank, or secure us against future suspensions.[51]

James Guthrie, immediate predecessor of Howell Cobb, had expressed himself in no uncertain language upon the laxity of the state governments in their regulation of note issues. He contended that if the states continued the policy Congress would be justified in levying a tax on the notes that would in effect abrogate the power.[52]

It was left, however, for Salmon P. Chase, one of our most competent Secretaries of the Treasury, to revive the question of the legality of state banknotes and to begin the prepara-

[51] *First Annual Message*, Dec. 8, 1857. See Richardson, *op. cit.*, V, 440.

[52] *Report of the Secretary of Treas.*, Dec., 1855, *Finance Report.*

tion of a radical change which finally culminated in the passage of the National Banking Act of 1863. Said he, in his report on the finances in 1861:

It has been well questioned by the most eminent statesmen whether a currency of bank notes issued by local institutions under state laws, is not, in fact, prohibited by the national constitution. Such emissions certainly fall within the spirit if not within the letter of the constitutional prohibition of the emission of bills of credit by the states, and of making by them of anything except gold and silver coin a legal tender in payments of debt.

However this may be, it is too clear to be reasonably disputed that Congress, under its constitutional powers to lay taxes, to regulate commerce, and to regulate the value of coin, possesses ample authority to control the credit circulation which enters so largely into the transactions of commerce, and affects in so many ways the value of coin. In the judgment of the Secretary the time has arrived when Congress should exercise this authority. . . .[53]

Any attempt at a detailed account of the steps leading up to the passage of the National Banking Act or an analysis of the act itself would be considerably beyond the limits we have set for this book. It is our intention merely to point out that the panic of 1857, in high-lighting the evils of a hopelessly confused banking and currency system, set the stage for a reform which would doubtless have occurred, even had the Civil War never served to hasten it.

The prevailing motive which dominated Mr. Chase throughout the struggle [says Davis] was the desire to secure a uniform currency which should be more controllable than would be government notes emitted for the same purpose. His method of obtaining this currency brought with it the benefit to the market for bonds, the securing of depositories and fiscal agents, and, above all, the guaranty that in future there should be no banks capable of furnishing credit to revolting states.[54]

One remedy—a great favorite with some—which was urged upon the government was protectionism. Its most zealous ad-

[53] *Finance Report,* 1861.

[54] A. M. Davis, *The Origin of the National Banking System,* p. 112.

vocates, Horace Greeley and Henry C. Carey, eloquently and unceasingly urged the Buchanan administration to increase custom duties. Such an increase, they insisted, would free the country of excessive imports and dependence upon outsiders. Moreover, it would relieve the Treasury of financial embarrassment. A higher tariff, they maintained, would mean the erection of new factories, furnaces, and so forth, which would "give employment to thousands of mechanics, artisans, laborers, who have for months languished in unwilling idleness." [55] Carey, even more persistent than Greeley, addressed a series of open letters to President Buchanan urging him to abandon free trade and adopt a policy of protectionism. Were this done, Carey declared, we would be relieved "of all further necessity for perusing the shocking accounts of poverty, despair, crime, and death with which our journals are now filled." [56] Nothing concrete came of these urgings, for the incidental protection recommended by Buchanan was blocked in the Senate and it was not until 1861 that the advocates of protection had occasion for rejoicing.[57]

[55] New York *Tribune,* Dec. 24, 1858, Jan. 20, 1859, March 11, 1859; *Harper's Weekly,* Oct. 10, 1857; *Bankers' Magazine,* XII, 849.

[56] Henry C. Carey, *Letters to the President on the Foreign and Domestic Policy of the Union;* also *Financial Crises, Their Causes and Effects,* pp. 18 ff.

[57] Richardson, *op. cit.,* V, 437, 440, 520 ff.; *Hunt's Merchants' Magazine,* XXXVII, 71; *Harper's Weekly,* March 13, May 15, 1858; New York *Tribune,* April 21, 1858.

CHAPTER SIX

CONCLUSION

FUNDAMENTALLY the causes of the panic of 1857 were not localized in the United States. Like all economic crises, it was an extremely complex phenomenon. Both long-time and short-time factors—domestic and international—contributed to its causation. A careful examination of world economic conditions during the ten years prior to 1857 leaves no doubt that the causes of the panic were as much or more European than American. Certainly the position of Great Britain in world economy has been too much slighted in the past in the treatment of American economic enterprise. And Great Britain's role cannot be comprehended unless one understands the far-flung economic relations between England and the rest of the world, particularly the Continent and more particularly France. This fact is of prime significance for the years preceding the panic of 1857. Indeed, anyone who endeavors to explain the panic of 1857 as something divorced and independent of what was transpiring in the Old World will be largely wasting his time. This must be obvious from the concluding pages of Chapter Three of this volume.

In making this statement we have no intention of slighting or belittling the short-time American factors. The credit structure of the United States was, at this time, weak and overstrained. A feverish get-rich-quick speculative atmosphere prevailed. The sudden increase in the world's gold supply by new discoveries in California and Australia had much to do with the inducement to inflation and speculation. Too much capital had gone into enterprises such as trans-Allegheny railroads, which yielded no immediate financial return. Unconcerned borrowing to sustain bankrupt and unprofitable projects was followed too rapidly by credit contraction and enforced liquidations.

The panic of 1857 has been usually charged to the failure of the Ohio Life Insurance and Trust Company, but this interpretation is superficial, for the failure of this particular concern was merely symptomatic of the state of American economy. When the Ohio Life Insurance and Trust Company closed its doors on August 24, 1857, the business interests of the country, instead of assisting the bankrupt organization to meet its obligations and thereby preserving the credit of the country, took fright. Banks suspended specie payment, in spite of the fact that they had in their vaults more gold than was necessary to redeem their paper notes. The absence of a central banking system and the fact that the federal government was incapable of interfering in the financial practices of the day, left the public without an authoritative guide to stem the tide of the crisis. Because of this, the fortunes of the Democratic party were to suffer, for the Buchanan administration was held responsible for a crisis which was not of its making.[1]

The Civil War, which needed a sound banking system in order to finance the army, once more raised the question of the legality of the state banknotes. States' rights in banking was now over. President Buchanan in 1857 laid at the doors of the banks a larger share of the causes for the panic than was actually justified. His proposal that gold and silver should be used outright and that the states issue currency only in large denominations can hardly be called a solution of the evil banking practices of the day.

Recovery, although traditionally regarded by historians as rapid after 1857, can hardly be justified in view of the factors

1 Luthin, Reinhard H., *The Background of Lincoln's Election to the Presidency*, Chap. I; Train, G. F., *Young America in Wall Street*, pp. 328 ff.

that arose. The country was not at all tempted to invest in real estate, mortgages, railroad stocks and bonds, notes of hand, and promises to pay debts. Greeley, reporting on conditions in the country at large, wrote that the crops were poor and railroads were not needed for transportation.[2] Although things looked brighter for 1859, on the morning of June 5 of that year the mercury dropped to 32 degrees and frost killed the wheat, corn, potatoes, vegetables, and fruits in New York, Ohio, Indiana, and Illinois. Thus unpredicted forces of nature contributed toward prevention of more rapid recovery.

What stands out as vitally significant in the panic of 1857 is that in a developing economy, such as was taking place in the United States, expanding forces do not for long remain in a state of equilibrium. The changes that were brought about because of the overexpansion in railroads and other enterprises and the halting of this expansion because of the panic helped to bring about a self-correction. Certainly the distress resulting from the panic had salutary psychological effects, even though these were temporary. Indeed some contemporary critics maintained that the panic and the resultant depression had taught men a new political economy: "That property resting . . . on a deceitful basis of fluctuating values, is among the least solid and permanent of all the things in which a man can invest himself. Material possessions lack the permanency of the spiritual." [3] The *Journal of Commerce* called upon its readers to "steal awhile away from Wall Street and every worldly care, and spend an hour about mid-day in humble, hopeful prayer." [4] One wonders whether this was the proper remedy for an economic disturbance, the causes of which transcended the boundaries of the United States, but it deserves serious thought.

[2] New York *Tribune*, Nov. 5, 1858.
[3] *Harper's Monthly Magazine*, XVI, 695.
[4] *Journal of Commerce*, Nov. 26, Dec. 2, 1857.

BIBLIOGRAPHY

THE MATERIALS for this study have been drawn from a wide variety of sources. The writer has leaned heavily upon the rich resources found in the Library of Congress, the New York Public Library, the Brooklyn Public Library, and the Library of Columbia University.

I. NEWSPAPERS

Albany Argus, 1857–58.
Brooklyn Daily Eagle, 1854–57.
Boston Advertiser, 1855–58.
Chicago Democrat, 1857–58.
Chicago Tribune, 1857.
Cincinnati Gazette, 1857.
Cleveland Plain Dealer, 1858.
Evansville (Indiana) Inquirer, 1858.
Indiana State Journal, 1857.
Louisville Courier, 1857.
National Era, 1858.
National Intelligencer, 1859, 1863.
New Orleans Picayune, 1857–58.
New York Evening Post, 1854–58.
New York Herald, 1854–59.
New York Journal of Commerce, 1857.
New York Times, 1854–59.
New York Tribune, 1854–60.
Ohio State Journal, 1858.
Philadelphia Ledger, 1858–59.
Philadelphia North American & United States Gazette, 1859.
Richmond Enquirer, 1858.
San Francisco Price Current, 1856.
St. Anthony Express, 1856.
St. Louis Republican, 1859.
Washington County (Wisconsin) Democrat, 1857.

II. PUBLIC DOCUMENTS

A. Federal

United States. Bureau of the Census. Census for 1850, 1860, 1880.

—— Eighth Census of the United States, 1864–66. 4 vols.

United States. Commissioner of Labor. Commissioner of Labor Report, 1886.

United States. Commissioner of Railroads. Annual Report. New York, 1899.

United States. Congress. House Executive Document, No. 20, 38th Congress, 1st Session.

—— Report on the Finances, Executive Document (Joint), No. 2, 36th Congress, 2d Session.

—— Senate Document, 36th Congress, 2d Session.

United States. *Congressional Globe,* 1856–57.

United States. Department of Agriculture. Resources and Industrial Conditions of the Southern States, by D. R. Goodloe, Report of the Department of Agriculture, 1865.

—— Statistical Abstract of the United States, 1890.

United States. Library of Congress, Division of Documents. Popular Names of Federal Statutes, 1926.

United States. Treasury Department. Annual Report of the Secretary of the Treasury on the State of Finances. Washington, 1857–59.

—— Report of the Secretary, 1850–60, in Congressional Documents.

United States. Treasury Department. Bureau of Statistics. Commerce of the United States with European Countries. Washington, 1893.

B. State

Illinois State Census Report, 1855.

Indiana Senate Journal and Senate Documents, 1857.

Michigan Senate Journal and Documents, 1856–57.

New York Senate and House Journal and Assembly Documents, 1857–59.

Ohio Senate Journal and Legislative Documents, 1857–58.

Statutes of the following states, 1857–60: Arkansas, Connecticut, Georgia, Illinois, Indiana, Kentucky, Massachusetts, Michigan, Missouri, New York, Ohio, Pennsylvania, and Virginia.

III. COLLECTIONS OF DOCUMENTS AND MAGAZINES

American Almanac, Vols. XV–XXXI. Boston, 1850–60.
American Railroad Journal. New York, 1857.
Bankers' Magazine. Baltimore and New York, 1850–60.
Cambridge Modern History, Vol. VIII. New York, 1907.
DeBow's Review. New Orleans, 1854–58.
Guide to the Illinois Central Railroad Lands. Chicago, 1860.
Harper's Weekly. New York, 1857.
Hunt's Merchants' Magazine, 1854–58.
Journal of Political Economy, Vol. IV. New York.
London Economist, January 11, 1851.
MacDonald, William, Select Documents Illustrative of the History of the United States. New York, 1908.
Magazine of Western History, Vol. II. Cleveland, 1884–94.
Minnesota Historical Bulletin. Minneapolis, 1917.
Moody's Magazine. Chicago, 1911.
Parliamentary Papers, Vol. V. 1857–58.
Poor, H. V., Manual of the Railroads. New York, 1881.
Report of the Mercantile Agency. New York, January, 1858.
Report of the Tappan McKillip Commercial Agency. New York, 1857.
Richardson, J. D., A Compilation of the Messages and Papers of the Presidents. New York, 1917. 10 vols.
Whig Almanac and Tribune Almanac. New York, 1851–60.
Williams, Edwin, Statesman's Manual. New York, 1858. 4 vols.

IV. GENERAL BIBLIOGRAPHY

Abbott, Lyman, Henry Ward Beecher. New York, 1903.
Adams, C. F., Richard H. Dana. Boston, 1890. 2 vols.
Baker, G. E., ed., Works of William H. Seward. New York, 1853–84. 5 vols.
Baker, H. F., Banks and Banking in the United States. Cincinnati, 1854.
Bancroft, Frederic, Slave-Trading in the Old South. Baltimore, 1931.
Bilbo, W. N., An Address on Banks and Banking. Boston, 1857.
Bishop, J. L., History of American Manufactures, 1608 to 1860. Philadelphia, 1864. 2 vols.
Blaine, J. G., Twenty Years of Congress. Norwich, Conn., 1884.

Bogart, E. L., The Economic History of the United States. New York, 1937.
Bolles, A. S., Financial History of the United States. New York, 1879. 3 vols.
Bross, W., Banking; Its History (Lecture). Chicago, 1852.
Brown, H. D., The Historical Development of National Expenditures. Washington, 1911.
Buchanan, James, Mr. Buchanan's Administration. New York, 1866.
Buck, Norman S., The Development of the Organisation of Anglo-American Trade. New Haven, 1925.
Bullock, C. J., Monetary History of the United States. New York, 1900.
Burton, T. E., Crises and Depressions. New York, 1917.
Caird, James, Letter on the Lands of the Illinois Central Railroad Company. London, 1857.
Camp, H. H., History of the Western Banks (Address before American Bankers' Association, at Saratoga, N.Y.). New York, 1879.
Cannon, J. G., Clearing Houses; Their History, Methods and Administration. New York, 1908.
Carey, H. C., Financial Crises; Their Causes and Effects. Philadelphia, 1864.
—— Money (Lecture). New York, 1857.
Carman, H. J., Social and Economic History of the United States, Vol. II. New York, 1934.
Channing, Edward, and Albert Bushnell Hart, Guide to the Study of American History. Boston, 1897.
Chase, S. P., Diary and Correspondence, in American Historical Association Report, 1902.
Cleveland, F. A. and F. W. Powell, Railroad Promotion and Capitalization. New York, 1909.
Cleveland, John, The Banking System of the State of New York. New York, 1857.
Cluskey, M. W., Political Text Book. Philadelphia, 1857.
Cole, A. C., The Irrepressible Conflict, 1850–1865. New York, 1934. Vol. VII of *A History of American Life,* edited by A. M. Schlesinger and D. R. Fox.
Cole, A. H., "Seasonal Variation in Sterling Exchange," *Journal of Economic and Business History,* Vol. II.
Colton, Calvin, The Life, Correspondence, and Speeches of Henry Clay. New York, 1857. 6 vols.
Committee of the Boston Board of Trade, Report, 1858.

Commons, J. R., and others, History of Labour in the United States. New York, 1918. 2 vols.
Conant, C. A., A History of Modern Banks of Issue with an Account of the Economic Crises of the 19th Century, 6th ed. New York, 1915.
Convention of the Northern Lines of Railway, Proceedings. New York, 1851.
Courtois, Alphonse, Histoire de la Banque de France. Paris, 1875.
Curtis, G. T., James Buchanan. Boston, 1883. 2 vols.
Daniel, J. W., "The Panic; Its Causes and Remedies," Speech in the United States Senate, Sept. 14, 1893, published in *Congressional Record.* Washington, 1893.
Daniels, W. M., American Railroads. Princeton, 1937.
Davis, A. M., The Origin of the National Banking System. Washington, 1910.
Depew, C. M., ed., One Hundred Years of American Commerce. New York, 1895.
Dewey, D. R., Financial History of the United States. New York, 1908.
Dixon, F. H., State Railroad Control. New York, 1922.
Dunbar, C. F., Extracts from the Laws Relating to Currency and Finance. Boston, 1891.
—— Economic Essays, O. M. W. Sprague, ed. New York, 1904.
—— The Theory and History of Banking. 3d ed. New York, 1917.
Dupont-Ferrier, Pierre, Le Marché financier de Paris sous le Second Empire. Paris, 1925.
Eames, F. L., The New York Stock Exchange. New York, 1894.
Evans, D. M., Commercial Crisis, 1857–58. London, 1859.
Everett, Edward, The Mount Vernon Papers. New York, 1858–59.
Foster, W. E., References to the History of Presidential Administrations. New York, 1885.
Fourtner, Samuel, Causes of Our Financial Panics. Seattle, 1908.
French, B. F., History of the Iron Trade. New York, 1858.
Fritz, Wilbert G., Contributions to Business-Cycle Theory; a Collection, Classification, and Reference Manual. Ann Arbor, Mich., 1934.
Frothingham, O. B., Life of Theodore Parker. Boston, 1874.
Gates, P. W., The Illinois Central Railroad and Its Colonization Work. Cambridge, 1934.
Gibbons, J. S., The Banks of New York; Their Dealers, the Clearing House, and the Panic of 1857. New York, 1858.
Ginzberg, Eli, The Illusion of Economic Stability. New York, 1939.

Greeley, Horace, The American Conflict. Hartford, 1864–67.
Haberler, G. von, Prosperity and Depression. Geneva, Switzerland, 1937.
Hadley, A. T., Railroad Transportation, Its History and Its Laws. New York, 1890.
Hammond, M. B., The Cotton Industry. New York, 1897.
Haney, L. H., A Congressional History of Railways. Madison, Wis., 1908.
Hart, A. B., American History Told by Contemporaries. New York, 1901–29.
Hazard, B. E., The Organization of the Boot and Shoe Industry in Massachusetts before 1875. Cambridge, 1921.
Hazard, R. G., Economics and Politics. Boston, 1889.
Helderman, L. C., National and State Banks. Boston, 1931.
Hepburn, A. B., History of Currency in the United States, rev. ed. New York, 1924.
Hibbard, B. H., A History of the Public Land Policies. New York, 1924.
Hildreth, Richard, History of the United States. New York, 1849–60. 6 vols.
Hirst, F. W., Six Panics and Other Essays. London, 1913.
Holst, H. von, The Constitutional and Political History of the United States, Vols. IV, V, and VI. Chicago, 1876–92.
Hooper, Samuel, Currency or Money. Boston, 1855.
—— Examination of Theory and Effect of Laws Relating to Specie in Banks. Boston, 1860.
Humphrey, E. F., An Economic History of the United States. New York, 1931.
Hutchinson, W. T., Cyrus Hall McCormick. New York, 1930–35. 2 vols.
Hyndman, H. M., Commercial Crises of the 19th Century. New York, 1892.
Jenks, L. H., The Migration of British Capital to 1875. New York, 1927.
Johnson, E. R., American Railway Transportation. New York, 1903.
Juglar, Clément, A Brief History of Panics and Their Periodical Occurrence in the United States, translated by D. W. Thom. New York, 1893.
Kettell, Thomas Prentice, Southern Wealth and Northern Profits. New York, 1860.
Larned, J. N., Literature of American History. Boston, 1902.

Lauck, W. J., The Causes of the Panic of 1893. Boston, 1907.
Laveleye, Émile de, Le Marché monétaire et ses crises depuis cinquante ans. Paris, 1865.
Liesse, André, Evolution of Credit and Banks in France. Washington, 1909.
Lunt, George, The Origin of the Late War. New York, 1867.
Luthin, Reinhard H., The Background of Lincoln's Election to the Presidency. In preparation.
McCulloch, J. R., Essays on Interest, Exchange, Coins, Paper Money, and Banks. Boston, 1850.
—— A Treatise on Money and Banks. Philadelphia, 1851.
McGrane, R. C., The Panic of 1837. Chicago, 1924.
Macgregor, John, Commercial Tariffs and Regulations, Resources, and Trade of the United States of Europe and America. London, 1846.
Mackay, Charles, Life and Liberty in America. New York, 1859.
McLaughlin, A. C., Lewis Cass. New York, 1891.
Manchester, Alan K., British Preëminence in Brazil. Chapel Hill, N.C., 1933.
Members of the New York Press, Panics and Revulsions in the United States. New York, 1857.
Meyer, B. H., History of Transportation in the United States before 1860. Washington, 1917.
Miller, H. E., Banking Theories in the United States before 1860. Cambridge, 1927.
Miller, S. L., Inland Transportation; Principles and Policies. New York, 1933.
Million, J. W., State Aid to Railroads in Missouri. Chicago, 1896.
Mitchell, D. W., Ten Years in the United States. London, 1862.
Mitchell, Wesley C., Business Cycles. Berkeley, Cal., 1913.
—— Business Cycles, the Problem and Its Setting. New York, 1927.
—— Business Cycles and Their Causes. Berkeley, Cal., 1941.
Morse, J. T., Abraham Lincoln. Boston, 1893. 2 vols.
Muhleman, M. L., Financial History of the United States from the Beginning of the Government. New York, 1908.
Myers, Sidney, Hard Times; Their Causes and Their Cure.
Oberholtzer, E. P., Jay Cooke, Financier of the Civil War. Philadelphia, 1907.
Perkins, D. W., Wall Street Panics, 1813–1930. Utica, N.Y., 1931.
Phelan, R. V., The Financial History of Wisconsin. Madison, Wis., 1908.
Phillips, U. B., American Negro Slavery. New York, 1918.

Ramon, Gabriel, Histoire de la Banque de France. Paris, 1929.
Rezneck, Samuel, "Depression and American Opinion, 1857–1859," *Journal of Economic History*, Vol. II.
Rhodes, J. F., History of the United States from the Compromise of 1850. New York, 1906–19.
Ringwalt, J. L., The American Transportation System. Philadelphia, 1888.
Ripley, W. Z., Railroads; Finance and Organization. New York, 1915.
Rogin, Leo, The Introduction of Farm Machinery in Its Relation to the Productivity of Labor in the Agriculture of the United States during the Nineteenth Century. Berkeley, Cal., 1931.
Russell, J. E., The Panics of 1837 and 1857 (Address). Boston, 1896.
Ryner, Ira, On the Crises of 1837, 1847, and 1857, in England, France, and the United States, "University of Nebraska Studies," Vol. V. Lincoln, Neb., 1905.
Sakolski, A. M., The Great American Land Bubble. New York and London, 1932.
Sanborn, J. B., Congressional Grants of Land in Aid of Railways. Madison, Wis., 1899.
Sandburg, Carl, Abraham Lincoln; the Prairie Years. New York, 1928. 2 vols.
Sanyal, Nalinaksha, Development of Indian Railways. Calcutta, 1930.
Sato, Shosuke, History of the Land Question in the United States. Baltimore, 1886.
Savage, John, Our Living and Representative Men. New York, 1860.
Schouler, James, History of the United States. New York, 1885–1913. 5 vols.
Schuckers, J. W., The Life and Public Services of Salmon P. Chase. New York, 1874.
Schumpeter, J. A., Business Cycles. New York, 1939.
Scott, W. A., The Repudiation of State Debts. New York, 1893.
Seward, William H., Works of, G. E. Baker, ed. New York, 1853–84. 5 vols.
Sheahan, J. W., Life of Stephen A. Douglas. Chicago, 1860.
Sherman, John, Recollections of 40 Years in the House, Senate and Cabinet. Chicago, 1895.
"Silex," Letters on Banks and Banking. Boston, 1853.

Stanwood, Edward, American Tariff Controversies in the Nineteenth Century. Boston, 1903. 2 vols.
—— A History of the Presidency. Boston, 1898–1912. 2 vols.
Stedman, E. C., The New York Stock Exchange. New York, 1905.
Stillman, J. D. B., Seeking the Golden Fleece. San Francisco, 1877.
Sumner, W. G., First Century of the Republic. New York, 1889.
—— History of American Currency. New York, 1884.
—— History of Banking in the United States. New York, 1896.
Taussig, F. W., State Papers and Speeches on the Tariff. Cambridge, Mass., 1892.
—— Tariff History of the United States. New York, 1890.
Thom, D. W., tr., A Brief History of Panics and Their Periodical Occurrence in the United States, by C. Juglar. New York, 1893.
Thorp, W. L., and H. E. Thorp, Business Annals. New York, 1926.
Thralls, Jerome, The Clearing House. New York, 1916.
Tooke, Thomas and William Newmarch, A History of Prices. London, 1838–57. 6 vols.
Train, G. F., Young America in Wall Street. New York, 1857.
Warden, R. B., The Private Life and Public Services of Salmon P. Chase. New York, 1874.
White, Horace, Money and Banking. Boston, 1896.
Wilber, E. J., A Treatise on Counterfeit, Altered, and Spurious Bank Notes. Poughkeepsie, 1865.
Williams, Henry, Remarks on Banks and Banking and the Skeleton of a Project for a National Bank. Boston, 1840.
Willis, H. P., History of Banking. Chicago, 1916.
Wilson, Henry, Rise and Fall of the Slave Power. Boston, 1872–74. 2 vols.
Wirth, Max, History of Financial Panics. Frankfort, Germany, 1883.
Wright, C. D., Industrial Depressions. Boston, 1886.

INDEX

Bei Fragen zur Produktsicherheit wenden Sie sich bitte an:
If you have any questions regarding product safety,
please contact:

Walter de Gruyter GmbH
Genthiner Straße 13
10785 Berlin
productsafety@degruyterbrill.com